All for Love

CHANDLER EDITIONS IN DRAMA
Robert W. Corrigan, *Editor*

John Dryden

All for Love

WITH AN INTRODUCTION

BY

R. J. Kaufmann

CHANDLER PUBLISHING COMPANY

124 Spear Street, San Francisco, California 94105

CONTENTS

INTRODUCTION

Seen through time's simplifying optical glass, John Dryden's life (1631-1700) has the same classical regularity and point as his verse. They are both of inspired consistency. Both show a power to respond to the larger tides of history without being swamped by them. His unmarked personal life is given form by his commitment to the problems of his time just as he gave form to these problems through his art. Born of sufficiently prosperous and unexceptional parents in Northamptonshire in 1631, Dryden's early environment was evidently Puritan. His intellectually formative years coincided with the turmoil of the English Civil War, a fact which early established his taste for order and for sensible restraint. In his mature role as poet, critic, physician to the ailing English language, and self-dedicated political conscience for his generation, he steadily earned the right to personify these needed traits of order, sense, and restraint, and he acted this role with imperturbable and unwaning eloquence. But the civil wars could not prevent a good education at Westminster and Cambridge, and Dryden during all of his successful life as a man of letters partly lived off the rich capital of classical learning he thus acquired. This prudent management of intellectual holdings is the hallmark of the true professional in the arts, and certainly as an artist and as a man Dryden was generous and careful at once. He possessed his own resources of image and allusion with the fullness of an eighteenth-century composer, and he reused them variously with the same bland, Handelian conviction of their durability.

This rich narrowness conditions his dramatic writing as it does all his poetry. So does his cultivated sympathy with the language and thought of classical Rome. Dryden eagerly shared the central Roman perception of the clear and definte properties of things, the Romans' creative legalism and indeed, their very notion of religion and art as *religio,* as that which regulates the collective spirit of the group and thus tames skepticism into retrospective piety.

The cycle of Dryden's inner growth, far from being a tricky matching of adjustable religious allegiances to political necessities, as was once alleged, can be seen by us as a growing identification of his private ethos with that of the two Romes—the Rome of Augustus Caesar and the Rome of the Holy See. Dryden needed to become a Roman Catholic for the same reasons that he had to spend three hard years at the height of his powers translating Virgil's *Aeneid*—a translation that is a triumph of articulate energy. It is also a sympathetic reclamation of an artist whom Dryden himself called "the plague of translators," who "seems to have studied not to be translated." A considerate reading of Dryden's Virgil is a splendid entryway to Dryden's views of things, for Virgil is preëminently the artist of the constructive will, of political discipline, of "that passionate affection for what has been achieved by blood and sweat, tears and misery, which men call patriotism" which patriotism in Virgil's as in Dryden's handling is very close to, though it never extinguishes, religious faith.

The other side of Dryden's skeptical, ironically distrustful, and antiromantic nature was fascinated by the bold, youthful inauguration of civilized order. The Virgilian celebration of heroic virtue as self-fulfillment through acceptance of the presiding will of Jupiter appealed deeply to Dryden. In this ethic the cautious, conservative side of Dryden's nature could be epically identified with the subordinate and fading heroic side—great deeds are done by Aeneas as an individual architect of order and as a selfless servant of his community. But Dryden did not achieve at one blow this Virgilian synthesis of material and supernatural ambitions any more than he was able to sacrifice without effort his affection for the willful egocentrics who populate the moral half-world of his heroic plays. The cathartic powers of art (particularly of dramatic art which nearly always has troubled conflicts of value at its heart) are greater and more varied than conventionally assumed.

Artists are often men who educate themselves in public and who make their audience intimate with their own soul's struggle for moral repose. So it was with Dryden. He was the first great English poet to operate from an initial central emptiness. He gradually filled in this inner void with persuasive doctrines; as his art unfolds we watch him do this. Wise men agree his special genius was for the satiric poetry which disciplines and instructs social belief. T. S. Eliot's fine assertion that "Dryden found the English speechless, and he gave them speech" properly refers to his moulding of a poetic idiom which makes possible civilized discussion of religious and political behavior and misbehavior in a fashion which transcends the triad of his predecessors' failings: obscurity, heavy didacticism, and vulgar abuse. This open, nervous, sufficient style of Dryden's was not a birthright—it had to be earned.

If we go to Dryden's Collected Poetry confident we can trace the smooth curve of growing mastery in this deliberate professional's work, we will be surprised. We find, instead, the unsteady verbalizings of Annus Mirabilis (1667) back to back with Absalom and Achitophel (1681), a masterpiece in prudent control and confidence. Between there is nothing for the uninstructed except an inference of fourteen years' silence. The truth, of course, is otherwise. Dryden spent the half generation between these two poems giving himself to the risky world of professional theater. We can no longer afford to look upon this as an unhappy turning away from his destiny as an artist—years of expensive error ended by his gratifying recall to his satiric vocation. He didn't go to the theater just to make money either, and we don't need his harsh exposés of compliant literary hacks to know that he was no poetaster whose liquid talents could flow unresistantly into every opportune social receptacle. Dryden was self-critical; the cumulative inadequacies of *Annus Mirabilis* as poetry constituted a mandate to this ambitious poet to develop a finer art. He did this in the poetic theater. It took a decade of concentrated effort from the circumscription of the issues in his great critical essay *Defense of Dramatick Poesy* in 1668 to the splendid consolidation of his mature poetic in *All for Love* in 1678. After that Dryden was ready. He remained a good, occasional dramatist while showing how greatness is possible in English satiric and controversial poetry in *Absalom, Religio Laici,* and *The Hind and the Panther.*

These well-known poems can receive nothing more than a salute here, but a brief consideration of what Dryden gained in the theater is desirable as critical preparation for *All for Love.* For it is beyond question that the drama raised and clarified the direct poetic voice he finally speaks in. The theater was not a detour for Dryden; it was a highroad to self. Despite his understandable resentment of the playwright's exposure to the thin, envious correction of sterile fools, he never wholly abandoned the theater. In fact, his last work, *The Secular Masque,* written a short time before his death, fuses with haunting clarity his satiric and his dramatic practice.

II

Dryden was thirty-one years old in 1662 when he wrote the first of his twenty-five or so plays: a comedy, *The Wild Gallant.* He was a clever man and a fertile one whose "thoughts, such as they are, come crowding in so fast upon me, that my only difficulty is to choose or reject." He was industrious and well-read in Classical, English, and French comedy. One of his comedies, *Marriage à la Mode* (1673) is still occasionally played. But despite the fact that some of these comedies join his heroic dramas in being "bad enough to please," as their author laconically stated, Dryden's gifts were not for stage comedy. He wasn't genial enough, and he cared too little for the affected world of social contingency. His lack of Shakespearean affection for unintelligent characters is not compensated for by the ingenious stage geometry of intrigue comedy, nor by the universal theatrical solvent of heavy sexual bawdry, and still less by his flogging of comic situation into farce and beyond it. Dryden's wit was great, but it was reflective and summary. He pondered and scored off; he portraited and epitomized—he looked for the disreputable essence of men and actions. Such wit is good for satire but not for comedy. Any comparison of Dryden's comedy to Jonson's, to Molière's, to Congreve's, instantly reveals the absence of ultimate respect for the form.

It is just as well. Restoration dramatists had problems. They lived under the shadow of Shakespeare and Jonson. They wrote for a small, self-consciously circumscribed group of privileged courtiers and their monied imitators. They were obliged to interpret the newly urbanized mind to itself. They were using actresses for the first time. They felt the heavy competition of French culture. They were uncertain about the proper language for their theater, since Fletcher's facility had taken the starch out of Elizabethan blank verse, while the heroic short-winded couplet put a low ceiling on tragic characterization. Prose was for comedy. In the division of artistic labors by the Restoration Dramatists, forging a critical comedy good enough to rationalize private motive and to stabilize a new sexual ethic short of rampant licentiousness and Hobbsian strife, fell to Etherege, Wycherley, and Congreve, all of whom were both gifted and interested. Congreve's culminating performance in this endeavor, *The Way of the World,* at once fulfills and exhausts the form.

Dryden's important work in the theater is in the so-called heroic play or heroic tragedy. He wrote a sequence of such plays, accompanied (for he was a self-critical and deliberate artist) by a series of discursive prefaces on the form. The earliest of his unaided performances is *The Indian Emperor* (1665), followed by *Tyrannic Love* (1669), the two-part *Conquest of Granada* (1669-70), *Aureng-Zebe* (1675) and climaxing in *All for Love* in 1678. Dryden wrote numerous other plays thereafter till the end of his life, but they display no sense of a continuing quest or design. His recasting of Shakespeare's *Troilus and Cressida* (1679) reveals much of the Restoration's temporal provincialism; his 1678 version of Sophocles' *Oedipus* has only its strangeness to recommend it. Some admire his *Don Sebastian* (1689-90), but the heart of his dramatic work—and it is work that profoundly affected subsequent English tragic writing—is in the heroic sequence climaxed by *All for Love.*

These plays form an organic cycle. They have a familial similarity in image and tone; they are obsessed by the same themes, and their fraternity of protagonists face similar moral threats. The intense episode of heroic plays (of which Dryden's are best) can be described historically as the death agony of the tragic drama in England, and as the last phase of Renaissance experimentation with high individualism. Thus these plays provide an obituary, somewhat hysterical perhaps, of tragic heroism as it had been understood. A heroism of service and *representative* initiative was replacing older conceptions of individual honor and *virtu,* but these more reckless forms of self-expression could not be given up without public ritualization—hence, heroic drama. The point is a crucial one. The grandiose and bombastic assertions of the heroes in Dryden's plays are not (as they are in Marlowe's *Tamburlaine,* or even in Ford's *'Tis Pity She's a Whore*) indications of the author's eager tribute to Promethean striving and its mission of radical social renovation. Almanzor, the apparently mighty hero of *The Conquest of Granada,* fights and slays thousands with his sword. His heady self-descriptions flood the play; "The minds of Heroes their own measures are,/They stand exempted from the rules of War" (IV, ii), and Dryden specifies in his preface he is to be thought of as having "an excessive and overboyling courage." Yet the lasting effect of the play is of inactivity, of too much leisure, of no true occupation, and of a constant effort at self-discipline rather than any expenditure of energy against the external world. Dryden, like Sartre in our time, is not truly political in his orientation, though he is obsessed with the consequences of political order and its negation, anarchy. There is something radically Stoical about Dryden's quest for the freedom of indifference. The description by the great Marxist critic George Lukacs of existentialist attempts at social critique as "a permanent carnival of fetishized inwardness" can be applied to Dryden's heroic plays as well. His orientation was psychological and personally redemptive. He had not the tragic writer's necessary belief in the constructive possibilities of the hero's defiance of a meaningful social order he must resist and which, by resisting, he redirects.

This incapacity to believe in the continuing social utility of heroic energy is what makes Dryden's plays less than high tragedy; it is also what makes them genuinely new and thus guarantees their lesser but definite importance as drama. There are two important points to make about this: one has to do with the dramaturgical consequences of *divided vision,* the other with the distinguishing features of what we can call *terminal tragedy.*

Dryden, the first great English critic, was a close student of the past dramatic literature of England. His conviction of Shakespeare's and Jonson's greatness was as free from provinciality as it was from envy; it was of a detailed professional texture and not of loose adulation. He studied their work. Tragic writing is a cultural and not merely a personal enterprise, and, through its fierce disputes, insights accumulate which are part of a national heritage. Tragedy seeks to embody adequately complex answers to adequately simple questions. Its quest is for root motives for action. As it matures through a tragic era, it develops an ever finer clinical technique for isolating and appraising the motivation of the protagonist. Thus tragedy slowly kills its own mystery in this perfection of technique and this achievement of "knowledge." Shakespeare's *Coriolanus,* for example, shows us clearly what can happen when a playwright grows too expert at disclosing real as opposed to disguised personal motive. Coriolanus's delusions about his own heroic independence are so easily exposed by Shakespeare's matured powers of analysis that he is reduced from tragic stature into "a boy of tears" tied mortally to his mother's will. What is gained in explicit psychological knowledge is lost in tragic respect and terror. Dryden was the beneficiary and the victim of this earlier achievement. The great issues had been searched into, motives had been anatomized. Dryden's mind was too conventional to question these discoveries. His genius was fluidly ironic and hence too accommodating to things as they are to transcend his skepticism of men's will to the good, or of their individual powers to hold out against the attractions of a pillowed throne or a soft bosom. Dryden's moral world was a hybrid of disenchanted political realism and romantic nostalgia.

This world promoted his divided vision, for he had a *satiric method* and *heroic memories*. The tragic vision tends to fall into these two parts when its era is ending. Thus, Dryden saw human faults clearly, and he brought to *separate* perfection the techniques for satirizing deluded motivation which were *inseparable* components of the complex attack of *Hamlet, King Lear,* or *The Duchess of Malfi.* The crucial other half of the tragic vision, the sense of human greatness actively transforming its world, is not so much lost as distanced into the past. Dryden did not deny heroism so much as he embalmed it, memorialized it in the form of terminal tragedy. His heroic stage was a museum of vital feelings honored lest they be forgotten, but securely preserved from present use.

Once freed from the camouflaging accidents of exotic detail, the indispensable, central situation of Dryden's heroic plays is of a dying emperor in the midst of a dying empire. His city is beleaguered and internal dissension is rife. Outside the gates "some strange beast, its hour come round at last" knocks rudely on the portals of history. Montezuma in *The Indian Emperor,* Boabdel in *The Conquest of Granada,* Aureng-Zebe in India, Cleopatra in Egypt, and the pagan, Maximin, vainly resisting in *Tyrannic Love* the irresistible triumph of Christianity, are all either literally "the last emperor" or are clearly understood as the descendant of an order once ascendant but now moribund, like strange races who lived before the Flood. Furthermore, Dryden chose heroes who are either superior or immune to normal social motives. They derive special strength either from an altogether foreign ethos—primitive Christian literalism, Islam, the apoliticality of the noble savage— or from worldly accomplishments, like Antony's, which are so definitive as to render indifferent any mundane claim of lesser degree than absolute love or absolute renunciation.

Dryden's recurrent images harmonize with his situations. He is addicted to terminal images of sunsets and twilight; of entropy, extinction and exhaustion; of sea monsters and antediluvian creatures left gasping on the strand; of water overflowing the land and forming lakes; of flat, undifferentiated things. This imagery reflects Dryden's own historical situation—one of gradual leveling of old distinctions, in the increasing democratizing of language and behavior. In the apprehension of the supersession of the old by the new, Dryden's sympathies were profitably at war with his critical awareness. His plays dramatize this conflict which is partly resolved in placing his central characters in remote, simplified, threatened societies with palpable enemies, so that heroic energies have clear employment but are clearly being replaced. Tribute is thus paid with no endorsement for the long future. Dryden's modern counterpart in this conflict is William Faulkner, whose southern aristocrats are individually intact and historically irrelevant. The disorder they live in is in direct contrast to the luminous exactitude of their memories. Against the huge world mindlessly engulfing them, they achieve momentary splendors of courage. Dryden's world is an engulfed world, and its ethos is precisely that reserved for those engulfed. Its logic and its absolute values are those of extreme situations. The appeal of his absolute solutions—religious conversion, suicide, and the like—is recognizably modern.

Dryden's society was demoting rugged individualism even as ours is. His serious drama is a critique of the unassimilable Achilles-Byron-Essex-Macbeth type of hero whose military skills are not helpful in a peaceful society and whose mind "is for a Calm unfit." Even the once heroic God is, in his plays, made remote and featureless until he is depersonalized into a figure admired but not loved, a God about whom one cannot be *enthusiastic*. Dryden thereby strips religious sentiment of its disturbing, heroic side effects while affirming its centrality. There is something very Virgilian about Dryden's Deity.

Dryden's special tone is reflected not only in his choice of heroes, situation, theme, and in his repertoire of images, but also in his conception of theatrical space and scene. Many must have noticed that he treats social values without giving us any convincing scene to set them in; his depiction of the political community is shadowy and hence exercises a shadowy claim to respect. Reflecting on this, we can see that his treatment of place is informatively different from the two writers whose dramatic handling of heroic material influenced him most—Corneille and Shakespeare.

Corneille worked out his theory of indeterminate place, *lieu théâtral*, so as to permit the inclusion of a variety of actions while still, nominally, adhering to the neoclassical demand of unity of place. Shakespeare, on the other hand, used place thematically, and hence abstracted motifs and characteristic qualities from Venice, Alexandria, a "blasted heath," or an enchanted isle as a means of conditioning his entire dramatic statement. He was interested in the qualities of a place as a supplementary means of dramatic significa-tion. But Dryden practiced a theory of *neutral space*. He wanted a character to be studied in relation to a particular set of conditions independent of his natural framing of a social setting. His heroes are insulated from external conditions by despair, defeat, cultural cataclysm, or by a world-negating philosophy. He drains space, in a quasi-scientific fashion, of all significance save that which he gives it for his own experimental purposes. His theater is an arena for psychological surgery; it is as free from distractions as possible.

III

Thus we can see that Dryden's theatrical style is deeply in har-mony with the Restoration stage with its new framing arch, its long diminishing perspectives, and hence its visual emphasis of isolated figures in the neutral space of a storied action.

To dominate such a stage required greatness. In the story of Antony and Cleopatra, and particularly in the figure of Antony, the epoch found its defining. figure, just as the Elizabethan theater had in Hamlet, the French Classical theater in Phaedra, and the whole western tradition in Antigone and Oedipus. Shakespeare had, of course, already treated the story with an autumnal completeness of language and insight. But his *Antony and Cleopatra* carries to their limits the panoramic tendencies permitted by the open, fluid Eliza-bethan stage and the wonderful power of thematic linkage through image and scenic echo still understood in Shakespeare's day but lost to the more rational procedures of Dryden's time and our own. It is conventional to make set comparison of the two plays, to the predictable disadvantage of Dryden. I do not think this is very fruitful. Dryden's sense of dramatic structure is closer to Ibsen's than to Shakespeare's. He stays close to the decisive moment of dramatic change. His *All for Love* is "one long catastrophe" and hence it limits the cast of characters, abbreviates the action, concen-trates effects, and formalizes character oppositions. Shakespeare's three great characters Enobarbus, Eros, and Ventidius all find in-carnation in Dryden's Catoesque bluff soldier Ventidius. Dryden's action takes place after Antony's humiliating flight from battle at Actium, a "moment of truth" which decided his life and, inci-dentally, sharply changed Western history.

If we define the climax of a play as the point after which no essential change can occur without flouting the structure of the action or contradicting the nature of the protagonists, it would be proper to say of *All for Love* that it is a retrospective tragedy in which the climax occurs before the action begins. There are a num-ber of advantages to this viewpoint. If everything has been decided, we are free to watch the fulfillment of "character as destiny," protected from any worries about externalities. And since something like despair has been achieved, the protagonists can be more open, they are past maintaining appearances. They are free to confront themselves, and this is exactly what Antony is made to do in *All for Love*. This gives the play the typical movement of those with a hero immobilized by sin, age, excess, metaphysical fatigue, or failure: plays like *Prometheus Bound, Oedipus at Colonus, Samson Agonistes,* and *The Masterbuilder*. These plays all stage a *psychomachia,* a war in the soul, and the lesser characters become to a degree expressions of competing parts of the conflicted mind of the suffering protagonist whose battle for freedom, for restored health, for self-comprehension—in short, for salvation from his self-induced mortal plight, is the action of the play.

In Antony, Dryden found a hero whose very brilliance in excess had more or less legitimatized itself through its grandeur, and whose faults others, looking upon this man of action's pathetic and helpless efforts at conscious appraisal of his moral responsibilities, are more ready to forgive than he is himself. For Antony has meant much to many others. He has seemed less subject to human limit than they themselves seem, and for each of them some part of his mighty and varied self has been an "all," an idealized whole. He has been generous with his courage, his virility, his high spirits, his goods, even with his innermost feelings. But his life has been a constant dynamic moving onward, and now he is stopped and all the wide-flung "lives" his potent nature have generated with and for others gather round him and are given voice. Here is an identity crisis not in adolescence but at the end of life. Cleopatra, Ventidius, Octavia, Dolabella—all—*know* him and try to recall him to his true self. Each one has a claim that is morally substantial and theatrically potent. This multiple invitation to renewal forms the confusing *agon,* the central struggle, of the play. The fact that all the lines of appeal run to a common center and that each one, while dignified in itself, is at odds with every other is part of the watchlike economy of this beautifully built play. One's sympathies are not easily brought to rest, evasive romantic identification with any one character is forestalled. But there are heavy risks, too, in this type of dramatic structure.

The neat externalizing of Antony's emotional commitments makes the contests *very* clear, but it makes him seem weak. There are almost no inner issues, no looming but obscure emotional dubieties. This accounts somewhat for the talky, artificial quality of the play. It isn't the conflicts themselves which are trivial, far from it, but that the conflicts seem to exist independently like disease entities—Antony doesn't seem to generate the conflicts out of himself but instead he contracts them one after another like maladies. These conflicts are classified according to expert emotional taxonomy of the period. Each confusion is to be got through, so that terminal immunity in the form of peace of mind can be achieved. Life, in this view, becomes a disagreeable means to an ulterior status. Hence, our vantage point is not—as it is in Shakespeare—from the midst of life outwards, but from a hypothetical, musing eminence beyond the action from which we look on these struggles of one who must remain forever in the past circumscribed in death by his own errors.

This sense of condescension to Antony is a symptom of an exhausted tragic vision. It is intensified by Dryden's immense inflation of the role of the eunuch, Alexas, the "atmospheric" bit player in *Antony and Cleopatra* raised to the magnitude of a stagemaster like Jonson's Mosca, manipulating the feelings and actions of his betters in *All for Love*. It is symbolically appropriate that in Dryden's revisionist view of tragic behavior the fate of the great lovers, themselves personifactions of dedicated sexual passion, should be determined by the non-man, the eunuch, Alexas, who represents, perhaps, the ingenious and metallic quality of reason unimpeded by any animal passion. Alexas, as developed by Dryden, shows both the resourcefulness of cold reason and its insufficiency. Alexas is bloodless, and his tidy and wholly selfish concern for his own literally sterile future is in deliberate contrast to the superabundant generosity of Antony, who "grows rich by giving" and the fecundity of Cleopatra's protean nature. It is, perhaps, too much to say that the world to come after such mighty figures of olden time, the great lovers and the soldiers who didn't count the cost, is to be a world dominated by the spiritual eunuchry of bureaucratic compromise and of prudence and intrigue, but it should be stressed that the most indicative change Dryden made in his reimagining of Shakespeare's play is the total exclusion of Octavius Caesar from the direct action.

Octavius's power is felt; he hovers over the action like Nemesis. The future belongs to him. By contrast Antony seems quixotic, obsolescent, tied to noble and unduly personalized confusions about the nature of historical reality. Part of the poignancy of Dryden's analysis derives from Antony's complete inability to grasp the nature of his opponent. The secure pragmatism of Octavius, his indifference to the opinion of others so long as his ends are served and his interests are unthreatened, combined with his freedom from any need to prove himself showily, his physical coldness and his instinct for the most economical way, make him virtually of another species than Antony. Dryden was wise not to put Octavius on the stage, for he is formidable as a representative of the inevitable future closing in upon and rejecting the Antonys of the world, but he would have been so colorless and unsympathetic on the stage as to have muddied Dryden's thematic intentions.

Dryden's Cleopatra is as far beyond standard stage portraiture as she is below Shakespeare's marvelous female. Dryden's Cleo-

patra reasons well enough to dislodge convictions far better an-
chored than Antony's, and the role should attract most good actresses within whose reach it readily falls. The scene between the
wronged Octavia and the threatened Cleopatra is a model of the
efficient staging of language. Dryden, whose own prudent marriage
to Lady Ann Howard was visited by little happiness, had a practiced ear for female argument. I think few modern readers will
subscribe to Dryden's judgment in his preface that "The greatest
error in contrivance seems to be in the person of Octavia." For,
though she must move compassion as he notes, there is no need in
the staging that her claim on Antony should seem any more ex-
clusively valid than those of the other competitors for his terminal
energies: Ventidius, Dolabella or Cleopatra herself. Only if we
completely disregard the possibility of nondomestic virtue, not to
say greatness, do we need to regret the telling use of Octavia.

In a brief introduction there is little room to speak of the healthy
clarity and controlled flow of Dryden's blank verse. It is a very
social poetry, full of succinct opinions to be shared and resting on
the rationalist's fiction that passions which agitate can be concur-
rently discussed by those they are agitating. There is little room,
too, to indicate how accurately the priest, Serapion, in the play's
first speech, catalogues the play's basic imagery and thereby pre-
figures the central theme: the overflowing Nile has left great antediluvian creatures panting on the shore. These "monstrous phocae"
are doomed survivals thrown up by the "fruitful Nile's" torrent.
They are fine imagistic equivalents for Antony and Cleopatra whose
o'erswelling passions and great natures are equally outmoded and
equally doomed. The play is close-wrought; the imagery and the
action qualify each other as they should in a poetic drama. Dryden
is the last great English poet who brought his mature skill to bear
as a working playwright in the professional theater.

In his rehandling of Antony's story, he brought to a circumscribed
perfection what the heroic tragedy could do. In *All for Love* Antony starts with all that other heroes seek—fame, honor, access to
beauty and power. He is a symbol; like a god he contains and
guarantees meaning for others. In a very precise sense the play
measures the mortality of his godhead and little by little, by matching his multiform meanings in the minds of his followers against
the mutable facts of his declining being, strips him of divinity and
of oversimple meaning and restores him to that special nobility
tragedy alone can give us—the felt essence of a man suffering en-
lightenment, thinking, and dying. This *recovery* of Antony's humanity is an imaginative feat. It brings with it a poignant realiza-
tion: a hero with sufficient brilliancy of character and achievement
to embody otherwise inaccessible ideals becomes necessarily the
disillusioner of others. They are betrayed by the seeming perma-

nence of this marriage in his person of the two realms of ideal and
fact which are otherwise separate. Here is a deeper, more moving
meaning for, "The best is enemy of the good," a meaning which
resolves the deepest conflict in Dryden's artistic character. If one
can believe that men of Antony's heroic stature are dead, that they
are obsolete, that nature no longer gives us such mirage-like creatures, then we can subside and there is a kind of peace—of rest
from struggle; the two realms are separate. What the artist can do
is to rejoin them retrospectively, and portray, in fixed works of art,
the time of their sacramental correspondence in that vanished world.
He need no longer seek for it in fact. He can elegize virtue, but he
need not explain it nor discern its workings in the fallen world. This
explains the "storied" quality of Dryden's plays; his many techniques of distancing, of abstracting. Such is the special quality of
Dryden's divided vision, such as the characteristics of this terminal
tragedy, *All for Love*.

R. J. KAUFMANN

University of Rochester
Rochester, New York

All for Love

CHARACTERS

MARK ANTONY

VENTIDIUS, *his General*

DOLABELLA, *his Friend*

ALEXAS, *the Queen's Eunuch*

SERAPION, *Priest of Isis*

MYRIS, *another Priest*

SERVANTS *to Antony*

CLEOPATRA, *Queen of Egypt*

OCTAVIA, *Antony's Wife*

CHARMION ⎫
IRAS   ⎬ *Cleopatra's Maids*
               ⎭

Antony's two little DAUGHTERS

PRIESTS, LICTORS, COMMANDERS, ATTENDANTS, EGYPTIANS, ROMANS

This version of *All for Love* follows the 1678 quarto, but modernizes spellings, typography, and punctuation throughout. A number of valuable suggestions for emendation have been drawn from J. H. Wilson's text.

PROLOGUE

What flocks of critics hover here today,   1
As vultures wait on armies for their prey,
All gaping for the carcass of a play!
With croaking notes they bode some dire event,
And follow dying poets by the scent.
Ours gives himself for gone; y'have watched your time!
He fights this day unarmed (without his rhyme)   2
And brings a tale which often has been told,
As sad as Dido's and almost as old.
His hero, whom you wits his bully call,
Bates of his mettle and scarce rants at all.
He's somewhat lewd but a well-meaning mind;   3
Weeps much, fights little, but is wond'rous kind;
In short, a pattern and companion fit
For all the keeping tonies of the pit.
I could name more: a wife, and mistress too,
Both (to be plain) too good for most of you;
The wife well-natured, and the mistress true.   4
   Now, poets, if your fame has been his care,
Allow him all the candor you can spare.
A brave man scorns to quarrel once a day,
Like Hectors, in at every petty fray.
Let those find fault whose wit's so very small,
They've need to show that they can think at all.   5
Errors, like straws, upon the surface flow;
He who would search for pearls must dive below.
Fops may have leave to level all they can,
As pigmies would be glad to lop a man.
Half-wits are fleas, so little and so light,
We scarce could know they live but that they bite.   6
But as the rich, when tired with daily feasts,
For change become their next poor tenant's guests,
Drink hearty draughts of ale from plain brown bowls,
And snatch the homely rasher from the coals,
So you, retiring from much better cheer,   7
For once may venture to do penance here.
And since that plenteous autumn now is past,
Whose grapes and peaches have indulged your taste,
Take in good part, from our poor poet's board,
Such rivelled fruits as winter can afford.

      8

ACT ONE

1   *[The Temple of Isis. Enter* SERAPION, MYRIS, PRIESTS *of Isis.]*

SERAPION   Portents and prodigies are grown so frequent
    That they have lost their name. Our fruitful Nile
    Flowed ere the wonted season with a torrent
    So unexpected and so wondrous fierce
2   That the wild deluge overtook the haste
    Even of the hinds that watched it. Men and beasts
    Were borne above the tops of trees that grew
    On th' utmost margin of the water-mark.
    Then, with so swift an ebb the flood drove backward,
    It slipt from underneath the scaly herd:
3   Here monstrous phocae panted on the shore;
    Forsaken dolphins there with their broad tails
    Lay lashing the departing waves; hard by 'em,
    Sea-horses, floundering in the slimy mud,
    Tossed up their heads, and dashed the ooze about them.

4   *[Enter* ALEXAS *behind them.]*

MYRIS   Avert these omens, Heaven!

SERAPION   Last night, between the hours of twelve and one,
    In a lone aisle of the temple while I walked,
    A whirlwind rose that with a violent blast
5   Shook all the dome; the doors around me clapped;
    The iron wicket that defends the vault
    Where the long race of Ptolemies is laid
    Burst open and disclosed the mighty dead.
    From out each monument, in order placed,
    An armèd ghost starts up: the boy-king last
6   Reared his inglorious head. A peal of groans
    Then followed, and a lamentable voice
    Cried, "Egypt is no more!" My blood ran back,
    My shaking knees against each other knocked;
    On the cold pavement down I fell entranced,
7   And so unfinished left the horrid scene.

ALEXAS *[showing himself]*   And dreamed you this? or did invent
    the story
    To frighten our Egyptian boys withal,
    And train them up betimes in fear of priesthood?

8 SERAPION   My lord, I saw you not,

Nor meant my words should reach your ears; but what   1
I uttered was most true.

ALEXAS   A foolish dream,
Bred from the fumes of indigested feasts
And holy luxury.

SERAPION   I know my duty;   2
This goes no farther.

ALEXAS   'Tis not fit it should,
Nor would the times now bear it, were it true.
All southern, from yon hills, the Roman camp
Hangs o'er us black and threating like a storm   3
Just breaking on our heads.

SERAPION   Our faint Egyptians pray for Antony;
But in their servile hearts they own Octavius.

MYRIS   Why then does Antony dream out his hours,
And tempts not fortune for a noble day   4
Which might redeem what Actium lost?

ALEXAS   He thinks 'tis past recovery.

SERAPION   Yet the foe
Seems not to press the siege.

ALEXAS   Oh, there's the wonder.   5
Maecenas and Agrippa, who can most
With Caesar, are his foes. His wife Octavia,
Driven from his house, solicits her revenge;
And Dolabella, who was once his friend,
Upon some private grudge now seeks his ruin;   6
Yet still war seems on either side to sleep.

SERAPION   'Tis strange that Antony, for some days past,
Has not beheld the face of Cleopatra,
But here in Isis' temple lives retired,
And makes his heart a prey to black despair.   7

ALEXAS   'Tis true; and we much fear he hopes by absence
To cure his mind of love.

SERAPION   If he be vanquished
Or make his peace, Egypt is doomed to be
A Roman province, and our plenteous harvests   8
Must then redeem the scarceness of their soil.
While Antony stood firm, our Alexandria
Rivaled proud Rome (dominion's other seat),
And Fortune, striding like a vast Colossus,
Could fix an equal foot of empire here.

                                                              9

1 ALEXAS   Had I my wish, these tyrants of all nature
      Who lord it o'er mankind, should perish—perish
      Each by the other's sword; but, since our will
      Is lamely followed by our power, we must
      Depend on one, with him to rise or fall.

2 SERAPION   How stands the queen affected?

  ALEXAS   Oh, she dotes,
      She dotes, Serapion, on this vanquished man,
      And winds herself about his mighty ruins;
      Whom would she yet forsake, yet yield him up,
      This hunted prey, to his pursuer's hands,
3   She might preserve us all; but 'tis in vain—
      This changes my designs, this blasts my counsels,
      And makes me use all means to keep him here,
      Whom I could wish divided from her arms
      Far as the earth's deep center. Well, you know
4   The state of things; no more of your ill omens
      And black prognostics; labor to confirm
      The people's hearts.

  [*Enter* VENTIDIUS, *talking aside with a* GENTLEMAN *of Antony's.*]

  SERAPION   These Romans will o'erhear us.
5   But who's that stranger? By his warlike port,
      His fierce demeanor, and erected look,
      He's of no vulgar note.

  ALEXAS   Oh, 'tis Ventidius,
      Our emperor's great lieutenant in the East,
6   Who first showed Rome that Parthia could be conquered.
      When Antony returned from Syria last,
      He left this man to guard the Roman frontiers.

  SERAPION   You seem to know him well.

  ALEXAS   Too well. I saw him in Cilicia first,
7   When Cleopatra there met Antony.
      A mortal foe he was to us and Egypt.
      But—let me witness to the worth I hate—
      A braver Roman never drew a sword;
      Firm to his prince, but as a friend, not slave.
8   He ne'er was of his pleasures; but presides
      O'er all his cooler hours and morning counsels;
      In short, the plainness, fierceness, rugged virtue
      Of an old true-stamped Roman lives in him.
      His coming bodes I know not what of ill
      To our affairs. Withdraw, to mark him better;
9   And I'll acquaint you why I sought you here,

And what's our present work.   1

[*They withdraw to a corner of the stage; and* VENTIDIUS, *with the other, comes forward to the front.*]

VENTIDIUS   Not see him, say you?
    I say I must and will.

GENTLEMAN   He has commanded,   2
    On pain of death, none should approach his presence.

VENTIDIUS   I bring him news will raise his drooping spirits,
    Give him new life.

GENTLEMAN   He sees not Cleopatra.
    3
VENTIDIUS   Would he had never seen her!

GENTLEMAN   He eats not, drinks not, sleeps not, has no use
    Of anything but thought; or, if he talks,
    'Tis to himself, and then, 'tis perfect raving.
    Then he defies the world, and bids it pass;   4
    Sometimes he gnaws his lip and curses loud
    The boy Octavius; then he draws his mouth
    Into a scornful smile and cries, "Take all,
    The world's not worth my care."

VENTIDIUS   Just, just his nature.
    5
    Virtue's his path; but sometimes 'tis too narrow
    For his vast soul; and then he starts out wide,
    And bounds into a vice that bears him far
    From his first course and plunges him in ills;
    But when his danger makes him find his fault,
    Quick to observe, and full of sharp remorse,   6
    He censures eagerly his own misdeeds,
    Judging himself with malice to himself,
    And not forgiving what as man he did,
    Because his other parts are more than man.
    He must not thus be lost.

    7
[ALEXAS *and the* PRIESTS *come forward.*]

ALEXAS   You have your full instructions, now advance;
    Proclaim your orders loudly.

SERAPION   Romans, Egyptians, hear the queen's command!
    Thus Cleopatra bids: Let labor cease;   8
    To pomp and triumphs give this happy day
    That gave the world a lord: 'tis Antony's.
    Live, Antony; and Cleopatra, live!
    Be this the general voice sent up to heaven,
    And every public place repeat this echo.

    9

VENTIDIUS [*aside*]   Fine pageantry!

SERAPION   Set out before your doors
The images of all your sleeping fathers,
With laurels crowned; with laurels wreathe your posts
And strew with flowers the pavement; let the priests
Do present sacrifice; pour out the wine
And call the gods to join with you in gladness.

VENTIDIUS   Curse on the tongue that bids this general joy!
Can they be friends of Antony, who revel
When Antony's in danger? Hide, for shame,
You Romans, your great grandsires' images,
For fear their souls should animate their marbles,
To blush at their degenerate progeny.

ALEXAS   A love which knows no bounds to Antony
Would mark the day with honors when all heaven
Labored for him, when each propitious star
Stood wakeful in his orb to watch that hour
And shed his better influence. Her own birthday
Our queen neglected like a vulgar fate
That passed obscurely by.

VENTIDIUS   Would it had slept,
Divided far from his, till some remote
And future age had called it out, to ruin
Some other prince, not him!

ALEXAS   Your emperor,
Though grown unkind, would be more gentle than
T' upbraid my queen for loving him too well.

VENTIDIUS   Does the mute sacrifice upbraid the priest?
He knows him not his executioner.
Oh, she has decked his ruin with her love,
Led him in golden bands to gaudy slaughter,
And made perdition pleasing. She has left him
The blank of what he was.
I tell thee, eunuch, she has quite unmanned him.
Can any Roman see and know him now,
Thus altered from the lord of half mankind,
Unbent, unsinewed, made a woman's toy,
Shrunk from the vast extent of all his honors,
And cramped within a corner of the world?
O Antony!
Thou bravest soldier and thou best of friends!
Bounteous as nature; next to nature's God!
Couldst thou but make new worlds, so wouldst thou give 'em,
As bounty were thy being; rough in battle
As the first Romans when they went to war;

Yet, after victory, more pitiful   1
Than all their praying virgins left at home!

ALEXAS   Would you could add to those more shining virtues,
His truth to her who loves him.

VENTIDIUS   Would I could not!
But wherefore waste I precious hours with thee?   2
Thou art her darling mischief, her chief engine,
Antony's other fate. Go, tell thy queen
Ventidius is arrived to end her charms.
Let your Egyptian timbrels play alone,
Nor mix effeminate sounds with Roman trumpets.
You dare not fight for Antony; go pray,   3
And keep your coward's holiday in temples.

[*Exeunt* ALEXAS, SERAPION. *Re-enter the* GENTLEMEN OF MARK
   ANTONY.]

SECOND GENTLEMAN   The emperor approaches and commands
On pain of death that none presume to stay.   4

FIRST GENTLEMAN   I dare not disobey him.

[*going out with the other*]

VENTIDIUS   Well, I dare.
But I'll observe him first unseen, and find   5
Which way his humor drives. The rest I'll venture. [*withdraws*]

[*Enter* ANTONY, *walking with a disturbed motion before he speaks.*]

ANTONY   They tell me 'tis my birthday, and I'll keep it
With double pomp of sadness.   6
'Tis what the day deserves which gave me breath.
Why was I raised the meteor of the world,
Hung in the skies and blazing as I traveled,
Till all my fires were spent, and then cast downward
To be trod out by Caesar?

VENTIDIUS [*aside*]   On my soul,   7
'Tis mournful, wondrous mournful!

ANTONY.   Count thy gains.
Now, Antony, wouldst thou be born for this?
Glutton of fortune, thy devouring youth
Has starved thy wanting age.   8

VENTIDIUS [*aside*]   How sorrow shakes him!
So now the tempest tears him up by the roots,
And on the ground extends the noble ruin.

ANTONY [*having thrown himself down*]   Lie there, thou shadow of
   an emperor;   9
The place thou pressest on thy mother earth

1 Is all thy empire now; now it contains thee;
Some few days hence, and then 'twill be too large,
When thou'rt contracted in thy narrow urn,
Shrunk to a few cold ashes. Then Octavia
(For Cleopatra will not live to see it),
2 Octavia then will have thee all her own,
And bear thee in her widowed hand to Caesar;
Caesar will weep, the crocodile will weep,
To see his rival of the universe
Lie still and peaceful there. I'll think no more on 't.
Give me some music; look that it be sad.
3 I'll soothe my melancholy till I swell
And burst myself with sighing.—

[*soft music*]

'Tis somewhat to my humor. Stay, I fancy
I'm now turned wild, a commoner of nature;
4 Of all forsaken and forsaking all,
Live in a shady forest's sylvan scene,
Stretched at my length beneath some blasted oak,
I lean my head upon the mossy bark
And look just of a piece as I grew from it;
5 My uncombed locks, matted like mistletoe,
Hang o'er my hoary face; a murm'ring brook
Runs at my foot.

VENTIDIUS [*aside*]   Methinks I fancy
Myself there, too.

6 ANTONY   The herd come jumping by me,
And, fearless, quench their thirst while I look on,
And take me for their fellow-citizen.
More of this image, more it lulls my thoughts.

[*soft music again*]

7
VENTIDIUS   I must disturb him; I can hold no longer. [*stands be-
for him*]

ANTONY [*starting up*]   Art thou Ventidius?

VENTIDIUS   Are you Antony?
8 I'm liker what I was than you to him
I left you last.

ANTONY   I'm angry.

VENTIDIUS   So am I.

9 ANTONY   I would be private. Leave me.

VENTIDIUS   Sir, I love you,   1
 And therefore will not leave you.

ANTONY   Will not leave me!
 Where have you learned that answer? Who am I?

VENTIDIUS My emperor; the man I love next Heaven;
 If I said more, I think 'twere scarce a sin— 2
 You're all that's good and god-like.

ANTONY   All that's wretched.
 You will not leave me then?

VENTIDIUS   'Twas too presuming
 To say I would not; but I dare not leave you, 3
 And 'tis unkind in you to chide me hence
 So soon, when I so far have come to see you.

ANTONY Now thou hast seen me, art thou satisfied?
 For, if a friend, thou hast beheld enough;
 And, if a foe, too much.   4

VENTIDIUS [*weeping*] Look, emperor, this is no common dew.
 I have not wept this forty years; but now
 My mother comes afresh into my eyes;
 I cannot help her softness.

ANTONY By heaven, he weeps! poor, good old man, he weeps! 5
 The big round drops course one another down
 The furrows of his cheeks.—Stop 'em, Ventidius,
 Or I shall blush to death; they set my shame,
 That caused 'em, full before me.

VENTIDIUS   I'll do my best. 6

ANTONY Sure, there's contagion in the tears of friends—
 See, I have caught it, too. Believe me, 'tis not
 For my own griefs, but thine.—Nay, father!

VENTIDIUS   Emperor!

ANTONY Emperor! Why, that's the style of victory; 7
 The conqu'ring soldier, red with unfelt wounds,
 Salutes his general so; but never more
 Shall that sound reach my ears.

VENTIDIUS   I warrant you.

ANTONY Actium, Actium! Oh!—   8

VENTIDIUS   It sits too near you.

ANTONY Here, here it lies, a lump of lead by day,
 And, in my short, distracted, nightly slumbers,
 The hag that rides my dreams.   9

1 VENTIDIUS Out with it; give it vent.

ANTONY   Urge not my shame.
 I lost a battle.

VENTIDIUS   So has Julius done.

2 ANTONY Thou favor'st me, and speak'st not half thou think'st;
   For Julius fought it out, and lost it fairly,
   But Antony—

VENTIDIUS Nay, stop not.

ANTONY   Antony,
   (Well, thou wilt have it), like a coward fled,
3 Fled while his soldiers fought; fled first, Ventidius.
   Thou long'st to curse me, and I give thee leave.
   I know thou cam'st prepared to rail.

VENTIDIUS   I did.

4 ANTONY I'll help thee.—I have been a man, Ventidius.

VENTIDIUS Yes, and a brave one; but—

ANTONY   I know thy meaning.
   But I have lost my reason, have disgraced
   The name of soldier with inglorious ease.
5 In the full vintage of my flowing honors,
   Sat still, and saw it pressed by other hands.
   Fortune came smiling to my youth, and wooed it,
   And purple greatness met my ripened years.
   When first I came to empire, I was borne
   On tides of people crowding to my triumphs—
6 The wish of nations! and the willing world
   Received me as its pledge of future peace.
   I was so great, so happy, so beloved,
   Fate could not ruin me, till I took pains,
   And worked against my fortune, chid her from me,
   And turned her loose; yet she came again.
7 My careless days and my luxurious nights
   At length have wearied her, and now she's gone,
   Gone, gone, divorced for ever. Help me, soldier,
   To curse this madman, this industrious fool,
   Who labored to be wretched. Pr'ythee, curse me.

8 VENTIDIUS No.

ANTONY   Why?

VENTIDIUS   You are too sensible already
   Of what you've done, too conscious of your failings;
9 And, like a scorpion, whipped by others first
   To fury, sting yourself in mad revenge.

I would bring balm and pour it in your wounds,
Cure your distempered mind and heal your fortunes.   1

ANTONY   I know thou would'st.

VENTIDIUS   I will.

ANTONY   Ha, ha, ha, ha!   2

VENTIDIUS   You laugh.

ANTONY   I do, to see officious love
Give cordials to the dead.

VENTIDIUS   You would be lost, then?

ANTONY   I am.   3

VENTIDIUS   I say you are not. Try your fortune.

ANTONY   I have, to th' utmost. Dost thou think me desperate
Without just cause? No, when I found all lost
Beyond repair, I hid me from the world,
And learned to scorn it here; which now I do   4
So heartily, I think it is not worth
The cost of keeping.

VENTIDIUS   Caesar thinks not so.
He'll thank you for the gift he could not take.
You would be killed like Tully, would you? Do,   5
Hold out your throat to Caesar, and die tamely.

ANTONY   No, I can kill myself; and so resolve.

VENTIDIUS   I can die with you, too, when time shall serve,
But fortune calls upon us now to live,
To fight, to conquer.   6

ANTONY   Sure, thou dream'st, Ventidius.

VENTIDIUS   No; 'tis you dream. You sleep away your hours
In desperate sloth, miscalled philosophy.
Up, up, for honor's sake! Twelve legions wait you   7
And long to call you chief. By painful journeys
I led them, patient both of heat and hunger,
Down from the Parthian marches to the Nile.
'Twill do you good to see their sunburnt faces.
Their scarred cheeks, and chopped hands.
There's virtue in 'em.   8
They'll sell those mangled limbs at dearer rates
Than yon trim band can buy.

ANTONY   Where left you them?

VENTIDIUS   I said in Lower Syria.

ANTONY   Bring them hither;   9

1   There may be life in these.

VENTIDIUS   They will not come.

ANTONY   Why didst thou mock my hopes with promised aids,
    To double my despair? They're mutinous.

2   VENTIDIUS   Most firm and loyal.

ANTONY   Yet they will not march
    To succor me. O trifler!

VENTIDIUS   They petition
    You would make haste to head them.

3   ANTONY   I'm besieged.

VENTIDIUS   There's but one way shut up.
    How came I hither?

ANTONY   I will not stir.

4   VENTIDIUS   They would perhaps desire
    A better reason.

ANTONY   I have never used
    My soldiers to demand a reason of
    My actions. Why did they refuse to march?

5   VENTIDIUS   They said they would not fight for Cleopatra.

ANTONY   What was 't they said?

VENTIDIUS   They said they would not fight for Cleopatra.
    Why should they fight, indeed, to make her conquer,
    And make you more a slave? to gain you kingdoms
6   Which, for a kiss at your next midnight feast,
    You'll sell to her? Then she new-names her jewels
    And calls this diamond such or such a tax;
    Each pendant in her ear shall be a province.

ANTONY   Ventidius, I allow your tongue free license
7   On all my other faults; but, on your life,
    No word of Cleopatra. She deserves.
    More worlds than I can lose.

VENTIDIUS   Behold, you powers,
    To whom you have intrusted humankind!
8   See Europe, Afric, Asia, put in balance,
    And all weighed down by one light, worthless woman!
    I think the gods are Antonies and give,
    Like prodigals, this nether world away
    To none but wasteful hands.

9   ANTONY   You grow presumptuous.

VENTIDIUS   I take the privilege of plain love to speak.   1

ANTONY   Plain love! Plain arrogance, plain insolence!
Thy men are cowards, thou, an envious traitor,
Who, under seeming honesty, hast vented
The burden of thy rank, o'erflowing gall.
O that thou wert my equal, great in arms   2
As the first Caesar was, that I might kill thee
Without a stain to honor!

VENTIDIUS   You may kill me;
You have done more already,—called me traitor.

ANTONY   Art thou not one?   3

VENTIDIUS   For showing you yourself,
Which none else durst have done? But had I been
That name which I disdain to speak again,
I needed not have sought your abject fortunes,
Come to partake your fate, to die with you.
What hindered me t' have led my conquering eagles   4
To fill Octavius' bands? I could have been
A traitor then, a glorious, happy traitor,
And not have been so called.

ANTONY   Forgive me, soldier;
I've been too passionate.   5

VENTIDIUS   You thought me false;
Thought my old age betrayed you. Kill me, sir,
Pray, kill me. Yet you need not; your unkindness
Has left your sword no work.

ANTONY   I did not think so.   6
I said it in my rage. Pr'ythee, forgive me.
Why didst thou tempt my anger by discovery
Of what I would not hear?

VENTIDIUS   No prince but you   7
Could merit that sincerity I used,
Nor durst another man have ventured it;
But you, ere love misled your wandering eyes,
Were sure the chief and best of human race,
Framed in the very pride and boast of nature;
So perfect that the gods who formed you wondered   8
At their own skill, and cried, "A lucky hit
Has mended our design." Their envy hindered,
Else you had been immortal, and a pattern,
When Heaven would work for ostentation's sake
To copy out again.   9

1 ANTONY   But Cleopatra—
Go on, for I can bear it now.

VENTIDIUS   No more.

ANTONY Thou dar'st not trust my passion, but thou may'st;
Thou only lov'st, the rest have flattered me.

2 VENTIDIUS Heaven's blessing on your heart for that kind word!
May I believe you love me? Speak again.

ANTONY Indeed I do. Speak this, and this, and this. [*hugging him*]
Thy praises were unjust, but I'll deserve them,
And yet mend all. Do with me what thou wilt;
3 Lead me to victory! Thou know'st the way.

VENTIDIUS And will you leave this—

ANTONY   Pr'ythee, do not curse her,
And I will leave her; though Heaven knows I love
Beyond life, conquest, empire, all but honor;
4 But I will leave her.

VENTIDIUS   That's my royal master;
And shall we fight?

ANTONY   I warrant thee, old soldier.
Thou shalt behold me once again in iron;
And at the head of our old troops that beat
5 The Parthians, cry aloud, "Come, follow me!"

VENTIDIUS Oh, now I hear my emperor! In that word
Octavius fell. Gods, let me see that day,
And, if I have ten years behind, take all;
6 I'll thank you for th' exchange.

ANTONY   O Cleopatra!

VENTIDIUS Again?

ANTONY   I've done. In that last sigh, she went.
7 Caesar shall know what 'tis to force a lover
From all he holds most dear.

VENTIDIUS   Methinks you breathe
Another soul. Your looks are more divine;
You speak a hero, and you move a god.

8 ANTONY Oh, thou hast fired me! My soul's up in arms,
And mans each part about me. Once again
That noble eagerness of fight has seized me,
That eagerness with which I darted upward
To Cassius' camp. In vain the steepy hill
9 Opposed my way; in vain a war of spears

Sung round my head and planted all my shield;   1
I won the trenches while my foremost men
Lagged on the plain below.

VENTIDIUS   Ye gods, ye gods,
For such another hour!

ANTONY   Come on, my soldier!   2
Our hearts and arms are still the same. I long
Once more to meet our foes, that thou and I,
Like time and death, marching before our troops,
May taste fate to them, mow them out a passage,
And, entering where the foremost squadrons yield,
Begin the noble harvest of the field.   3

[*Exeunt.*]

ACT TWO

1 [*Enter* CLEOPATRA, IRAS, *and* ALEXAS.]

CLEOPATRA   What shall I do or whither shall I turn?
Ventidius has o'ercome, and he will go.

ALEXAS   He goes to fight for you.

2 CLEOPATRA   Then he would see me ere he went to fight.
Flatter me not. If once he goes, he's lost,
And all my hopes destroyed.

ALEXAS   Does this weak passion
Become a mighty queen?

3 CLEOPATRA   I am no queen.
Is this to be a queen, to be besieged
By yon insulting Roman, and to wait
Each hour the victor's chain? These ills are small;
For Antony is lost, and I can mourn
For nothing else but him. Now come, Octavius,
4 I have no more to lose! Prepare thy bands;
I'm fit to be a captive; Antony
Has taught my mind the fortune of a slave.

IRAS   Call reason to assist you.

5 CLEOPATRA   I have none,
And none would have. My love's a noble madness,
Which shows the cause deserved it. Moderate sorrow
Fits vulgar love, and for a vulgar man,
But I have loved with such transcendent passion,
I soared, at first, quite out of reason's view,
6 And now am lost above it. No, I'm proud
'Tis thus. Would Antony could see me now!
Think you he would not sigh? Though he must leave me,
Sure, he would sigh, for he is noble-natured,
And bears a tender heart. I know him well.
Ah, no, I know him not; I knew him once,
7 But now 'tis past.

IRAS   Let it be past with you.
Forget him, madam.

CLEOPATRA   Never, never, Iras.
8 He once was mine; and once, though now 'tis gone,
Leaves a faint image of possession still.

18

ALEXAS   Think him unconstant, cruel, and ungrateful.   1

CLEOPATRA   I cannot. If I could, those thoughts were vain.
Faithless, ungrateful, cruel though he be,
I still must love him.

[*Enter* CHARMION]   2
                              Now, what news, my Charmion?
Will he be kind? And will he not forsake me?
Am I to live, or die?—nay, do I live?
Or am I dead? For when he gave his answer,
Fate took the word, and then I lived or died.
                                                                          3
CHARMION   I found him, madam—

CLEOPATRA   A long speech preparing?
If thou bring'st comfort, haste, and give it me,
For never was more need.

IRAS   I know he loves you.
                                                                          4
CLEOPATRA   Had he been kind, her eyes had told me so
Before her tongue could speak it. Now she studies
To soften what he said; but give me death
Just as he sent it, Charmion, undisguised,
And in the words he spoke.
                                                                          5
CHARMION   I found him, then,
Encompassed round, I think, with iron statues;
So mute, so motionless his soldiers stood,
While awfully he cast his eyes about
And every leader's hopes or fears surveyed.
Methought he looked resolved, and yet not pleased.   6
When he beheld me struggling in the crowd,
He blushed, and bade make way.

ALEXAS   There's comfort yet.

CHARMION   Ventidius fixed his eyes upon my passage   7
Severely, as he meant to frown me back,
And sullenly gave place. I told my message,
Just as you gave it, broken and disordered;
I numbered in it all your sighs and tears,
And while I moved your pitiful request,
That you but only begged a last farewell,   8
He fetched an inward groan; and every time
I named you, sighed as if his heart were breaking,
But shunned my eyes and guiltily looked down.
He seemed not now that awful Antony
Who shook an armed assembly with his nod;
But, making show as he would rub his eyes,   9

1   Disguised and blotted out a falling tear.

CLEOPATRA   Did he then weep? And was I worth a tear?
If what thou hast to say be not as pleasing,
Tell me no more, but let me die contented.

CHARMION   He bid me say, he knew himself so well,
2   He could deny you nothing if he saw you;
And therefore—

CLEOPATRA   Thou wouldst say, he would not see me?

CHARMION   And therefore begged you not to use a power
Which he could ill resist; yet he should ever
3   Respect you as he ought.

CLEOPATRA   Is that a word
For Antony to use to Cleopatra?
O that faint word, *respect!* how I disdain it!
Disdain myself for loving, after it!
4   He should have kept that word for cold Octavia.
Respect is for a wife. Am I that thing,
That dull, insipid lump, without desires,
And without power to give them?

ALEXAS   You misjudge;
You see through love, and that deludes your sight,
5   As what is straight seems crooked through the water.
But I, who bear my reason undisturbed,
Can see this Antony, this dreaded man,
A fearful slave who fain would run away,
And shuns his master's eyes. If you pursue him,
6   My life on 't, he still drags a chain along
That needs must clog his flight.

CLEOPATRA   Could I believe thee!—

ALEXAS   By every circumstance I know he loves,
True, he's hard pressed by int'rest and by honor;
7   Yet he but doubts and parleys and casts out
Many a long look for succor.

CLEOPATRA   He sends word
He fears to see my face.

ALEXAS   And would you more?
8   He shows his weakness who declines the combat,
And you must urge your fortune. Could he speak
More plainly? To my ears the message sounds—
"Come to my rescue, Cleopatra, come;
Come, free me from Ventidius—from my tyrant;
9   See me and give me a pretense to leave him!"

I hear his trumpets. This way he must pass.
Please you, retire a while; I'll work him first,
That he may bend more easy.

CLEOPATRA   You shall rule me;
But all, I fear, in vain.

[*Exit with* CHARMION *and* IRAS.]

ALEXAS   I fear so, too,
Though I concealed my thoughts, to make her bold,
But 'tis our utmost means, and fate befriend it! [*withdraws*]

[*Enter* LICTORS *with fasces, one bearing the eagle; then enter*
ANTONY *with* VENTIDIUS, *followed by other* COMMANDERS.]

ANTONY   Octavius is the minion of blind chance
But holds from virtue nothing.

VENTIDIUS   Has he courage?

ANTONY   But just enough to season him from coward.
Oh, 'tis the coldest youth upon a charge,
The most deliberate fighter! If he ventures
(As in Illyria once, they say, he did,
To storm a town), 'tis when he cannot choose;
When all the world have fixed their eyes upon him,
And then he lives on that for seven years after;
But at a close revenge he never fails.

VENTIDIUS   I heard you challenged him.

ANTONY   I did, Ventidius.
What think'st thou was his answer? 'Twas so tame!—
He said he had more ways than one to die;
I had not.

VENTIDIUS   Poor!

ANTONY   He has more ways than one,
But he would chose them all before that one.

VENTIDIUS   He first would choose an ague or a fever.

ANTONY   No; it must be an ague, not a fever;
He has not warmth enough to die by that.

VENTIDIUS   Or old age and a bed.

ANTONY   Ay, there's his choice,
He would live like a lamp to the last wink,
And crawl upon the utmost verge of life.
O Hercules! Why should a man like this,
Who dares not trust his fate for one great action,
Be all the care of Heaven? Why should he lord it

1 O'er fourscore thousand men, of whom each one
Is braver than himself?

VENTIDIUS   You conquered for him.
Philippi knows it; there you shared with him
That empire which your sword made all your own.

2 ANTONY   Fool that I was, upon my eagle's wings
I bore this wren till I was tired with soaring,
And now he mounts above me.
Good heavens, is this—is this the man who braves me?
Who bids my age make way? Drives me before him
To the world's ridge and sweeps me off like rubbish?

3 VENTIDIUS   Sir, we lose time; the troops are mounted all.

ANTONY   Then give the word to march.
I long to leave this prison of a town,
To join thy legions, and in open field
4 Once more to show my face. Lead, my deliverer.

[*Enter* ALEXAS.]

ALEXAS   Great emperor,
In mighty arms renowned above mankind,
But in soft pity to th' oppressed, a god,
5 This message sends the mournful Cleopatra
To her departing lord.

VENTIDIUS   Smooth sycophant!

ALEXAS   A thousand wishes and ten thousand prayers,
Millions of blessings wait you to the wars;
6 Millions of sighs and tears she sends you, too,
And would have sent
As many dear embraces to your arms,
As many parting kisses to your lips,
But those, she fears, have wearied you already.

7 VENTIDIUS [*aside*]   False crocodile!

ALEXAS   And yet she begs not now you would not leave her;
That were a wish too mighty for her hopes,
Too presuming
For her low fortune and your ebbing love;
That were a wish for her more prosperous days,
8 Her blooming beauty and your growing kindness.

ANTONY [*aside*]   Well, I must man it out.—What would the queen?

ALEXAS   First, to these noble warriors who attend
Your daring courage in the chase of fame,—
9 Too daring and too dangerous for her quiet,—

She humbly recommends all she holds dear,   1
All her own cares and fears,—the care of you.

VENTIDIUS   Yes, witness Actium.

ANTONY   Let him speak, Ventidius.

ALEXAS   You, when his matchless valor bears him forward
With ardor too heroic, on his foes,   2
Fall down, as she would do, before his feet;
Lie in his way and stop the paths of death.
Tell him this god is not invulnerable,
That absent Cleopatra bleeds in him,
And, that you may remember her petition,   3
She begs you wear these trifles as a pawn
Which, at your wished return, she will redeem [*gives jewels to the*
    COMMANDERS]
With all the wealth of Egypt.
This to the great Ventidius she presents,
Whom she can never count her enemy,   4
Because he loves her lord.

VENTIDIUS   Tell her, I'll none on 't;
I'm not ashamed of honest poverty;
Not all the diamonds of the east can bribe
Ventidius from his faith. I hope to see   5
These and the rest of all her sparkling store
Where they shall more deservingly be placed.

ANTONY   And who must wear 'em then?

VENTIDIUS   The wronged Octavia.

ANTONY   You might have spared that word.   6

VENTIDIUS   And he, that bribe.

ANTONY   But have I no remembrance?

ALEXAS   Yes, a dear one;
Your slave the queen—   7

ANTONY   My mistress.

ALEXAS   Then your mistress;
Your mistress would, she says, have sent her soul,
But that you had long since; she humbly begs
This ruby bracelet, set with bleeding hearts,   8
The emblems of her own, may bind your arm. [*presenting a
    bracelet*]

VENTIDIUS   Now, my best lord, in honor's name, I ask you,
For manhood's sake and for your own dear safety,
Touch not these poisoned gifts,   9

1 Infected by the sender; touch 'em not;
Myriads of bluest plagues lie underneath them,
And more than aconite has dipped the silk.

ANTONY   Nay, now you grow too cynical, Ventidius;
A lady's favors may be worn with honor.
2 What, to refuse her bracelet! On my soul,
When I lie pensive in my tent alone,
'Twill pass the wakeful hours of winter nights.
To tell these pretty beads upon my arm,
To count for every one a soft embrace,
A melting kiss at such and such a time,
3 And now and then the fury of her love
When—And what harm's in this?

ALEXAS   None, none, my lord,
But what's to her, that now 'tis past forever.

ANTONY [*going to tie it*]   We soldiers are so awkward—help me
4   tie it.

ALEXAS   In faith, my lord, we courtiers, too, are awkward
In these affairs; so are all men indeed,
Even I, who am not one. But shall I speak?

ANTONY   Yes, freely.
5
ALEXAS   Then, my lord, fair hands alone
Are fit to tie it; she who sent it can.

VENTIDIUS   Hell! death! this eunuch pander ruins you.
You will not see her?

6 [ALEXAS *whispers to an* ATTENDANT, *who goes out.*]

ANTONY   But to take my leave.

VENTIDIUS   Then I have washed an Aethiop. You're undone;
You're in the toils; you're taken; you're destroyed;
Her eyes do Caesar's work.
7
ANTONY   You fear too soon.
I'm constant to myself; I know my strength;
And yet she shall not think me barbarous neither,
Born in the depths of Afric. I'm a Roman,
Bred to the rules of soft humanity.
8 A guest, and kindly used, should bid farewell.

VENTIDIUS   You do not know
How weak you are to her, how much an infant;
You are not proof against a smile or glance;
A sigh will quite disarm you.

9 ANTONY   See, she comes!
Now you shall find your error.—Gods, I thank you.

I formed the danger greater than it was,
And now 'tis near, 'tis lessened.

VENTIDIUS   Mark the end yet.

[*Enter* CLEOPATRA, CHARMION, *and* IRAS.]

ANTONY   Well, madam, we are met.

CLEOPATRA   Is this a meeting?
Then, we must part?

ANTONY   We must.

CLEOPATRA   Who says we must?

ANTONY   Our own hard fates.

CLEOPATRA   We make those fates ourselves.

ANTONY   Yes, we have made them; we have loved each other
Into our mutual ruin.

CLEOPATRA   The gods have seen my joys with envious eyes;
I have no friends in heaven, and all the world,
As 'twere the business of mankind to part us,
Is armed against my love. Even you yourself
Join with the rest; you, you are armed against me.

ANTONY   I will be justified in all I do
To late posterity, and therefore hear me.
If I mix a lie
With any truth, reproach me freely with it;
Else, favor me with silence.

CLEOPATRA   You command me,
And I am dumb.

VENTIDIUS [*aside*]   I like this well; he shows authority.

ANTONY   That I derive my ruin
From you alone—

CLEOPATRA   O heavens! I ruin you!

ANTONY   You promised me your silence, and you break it
Ere I have scarce begun.

CLEOPATRA   Well, I obey you.

ANTONY   When I beheld you first, it was in Egypt.
Ere Caesar saw your eyes, you gave me love,
And were too young to know it; that I settled
Your father in his throne was for your sake;
I left th' acknowledgment for time to ripen.
Caesar stepped in and with a greedy hand
Plucked the green fruit ere the first blush of red,
Yet cleaving to the bough. He was my lord,

1 And was, beside, too great for me to rival.
   But I deserved you first, though he enjoyed you.
   When, after, I beheld you in Cilicia,
   An enemy to Rome, I pardoned you.

   CLEOPATRA   I cleared myself—

2 ANTONY   Again you break your promise.
   I loved you still and took your weak excuses,
   Took you into my bosom, stained by Caesar,
   And not half mine. I went to Egypt with you,
   And hid me from the business of the world,
   Shut out inquiring nations from my sight
3 To give whole years to you.

   VENTIDIUS [aside]   Yes, to your shame be 't spoken.

   ANTONY   How I loved,
   Witness, ye days and nights and all your hours
   That danced away with down upon your feet,
4 As all your business were to count my passion!
   One day passed by and nothing saw but love;
   Another came and still 'twas only love.
   The suns were wearied out with looking on,
   And I untired with loving.
5 I saw you every day, and all the day;
   And every day was still but as the first,
   So eager was I still to see you more.

   VENTIDIUS   'Tis all too true.

   ANTONY   Fulvia, my wife, grew jealous,
6 As she indeed had reason; raised a war
   In Italy to call me back.

   VENTIDIUS   But yet
   You went not.

   ANTONY   While within your arms I lay,
7 The world fell moldering from my hands each hour,
   And left me scarce a grasp—I thank your love for 't.

   VENTIDIUS   Well pushed: that last was home.

   CLEOPATRA   Yet may I speak?

8 ANTONY   If I have urged a falsehood, yes; else, not.
   Your silence says I have not. Fulvia died
   (Pardon, you gods, with my unkindness died);
   To set the world at peace I took Octavia,
   This Caesar's sister; in her pride of youth
   And flower of beauty did I wed that lady,
9 Whom, blushing, I must praise, because I left her.
   You called; my love obeyed the fatal summons.

This raised the Roman arms; the cause was yours,　　　　　1
I would have fought by land where I was stronger;
You hindered it; yet, when I fought at sea,
Forsook me fighting; and (O stain to honor!
O lasting shame!) I knew not that I fled,
But fled to follow you.

VENTIDIUS　　What haste she made to hoist her purple sails!　　2
　　And, to appear magnificent in flight,
　　Drew half our strength away.

ANTONY　　　　　　　　　　All this you caused.
　　And would you multiply more ruins on me?
　　This honest man, my best, my only friend,　　　　　3
　　Has gathered up the shipwreck of my fortunes;
　　Twelve legions I have left, my last recruits,
　　And you have watched the news, and bring your eyes
　　To seize them, too. If you have aught to answer.
　　Now speak, you have free leave.　　　　　　　4

ALEXAS [aside]　　She stands confounded.
　　Despair is in her eyes.

VENTIDIUS　　Now lay a sigh i' th' way to stop his passage;
　　Prepare a tear and bid it for his legions;
　　'Tis like they shall be sold.　　　　　　　5

CLEOPATRA　　How shall I plead my cause when you, my judge,
　　Already have condemned me? Shall I bring
　　The love you bore me for my advocate?
　　That now is turned against me, that destroys me;
　　For love, once past, is, at the best, forgotten,　　　6
　　But oft'ner sours to hate. 'Twill please my lord
　　To ruin me, and therefore I'll be guilty.
　　But could I once have thought it would have pleased you,
　　That you would pry, with narrow searching eyes,
　　Into my faults, severe to my destruction,
　　And watching all advantages with care　　　　　7
　　That serve to make me wretched? Speak, my lord,
　　For I end here. Though I deserve this usage,
　　Was it like you to give it?

ANTONY　　　　　　　　Oh, you wrong me
　　To think I sought this parting or desired　　　　8
　　To accuse you more than what will clear myself
　　And justify this breach.

CLEOPATRA　　　　　　Thus low I thank you,
　　And, since my innocence will not offend,
　　I shall not blush to own it.　　　　　　　9

VENTIDIUS [aside]　　　　　After this,

1   I think she'll blush at nothing.

CLEOPATRA   You seem grieved
(And therein you are kind) that Caesar first
Enjoyed my love, though you deserved it better.
I grieve for that, my lord, much more than you;
2   For, had I first been yours, it would have saved
My second choice: I never had been his,
And ne'er had been but yours. But Caesar first,
You say, possessed my love. Not so, my lord.
He first possessed my person: you, my love.
Caesar loved me, but I loved Antony.
3   If I endured him after, 'twas because
I judged it due to the first name of men,
And, half constrained, I gave as to a tyrant
What he would take by force.

VENTIDIUS   O Siren! Siren!
4   Yet grant that all the love she boasts were true,
Has she not ruined you? I still urge that,
The fatal consequence.

CLEOPATRA   The consequence, indeed,
For I dare challenge him, my greatest foe,
5   To say it was designed. 'Tis true I loved you,
And kept you far from an uneasy wife,—
Such Fulvia was.
Yes, but he'll say you left Octavia for me;—
And can you blame me to receive that love
Which quitted such desert for worthless me?
6   How often have I wished some other Caesar,
Great as the first, and as the second, young,
Would court my love to be refused for you!

VENTIDIUS   Words, words; but Actium, sir; remember Actium.

7   CLEOPATRA   Even there I dare his malice. True, I counseled
To fight at sea, but I betrayed you not.
I fled, but not to the enemy. 'Twas fear.
Would I had been a man, not to have feared!
For none would then have envied me your friendship,
Who envy me your love.

8   ANTONY   We're both unhappy.
If nothing else, yet our ill fortune parts us.
Speak; would you have me perish by my stay?

CLEOPATRA   If, as a friend, you ask my judgment, go;
9   If as a lover, stay. If you must perish—
'Tis a hard word—but stay.

VENTIDIUS   See now th' effects of her so boasted love!   1
   She strives to drag you down to ruin with her;
   But could she 'scape without you, oh, how soon
   Would she let go her hold and haste to shore
   And never look behind!

CLEOPATRA   Then judge my love by this. [*giving* AN-   2
   TONY *a writing*]
   Could I have borne
   A life or death, a happiness or woe
   From yours divided, this had given me means.

ANTONY   By Hercules, the writing of Octavius!
   I know it well; 'tis that proscribing hand,   3
   Young as it was, that led the way to mine
   And left me but the second place in murder.—
   See, see, Ventidius! here he offers Egypt,
   And joins all Syria to it as a present,
   So, in requital, she forsake my fortunes   4
   And join her arms with his.

CLEOPATRA   And yet you leave me!
   You leave me, Antony; and yet I love you,
   Indeed I do. I have refused a kingdom;
   That's a trifle;
   For I could part with life, with anything,   5
   But only you. Oh, let me die but with you!
   Is that a hard request?

ANTONY   Next living with you,
   'Tis all that Heaven can give.

ALEXAS [*aside*]   He melts; we conquer.   6

CLEOPATRA   No; you shall go. Your interest calls you hence;
   Yes, your dear interest pulls too strong for these
   Weak arms to hold you here. [*takes his hand*]
   Go; leave me, soldier
   (For you're no more a lover), leave me dying;   7
   Push me, all pale and panting, from your bosom,
   And, when your march begins, let one run after,
   Breathless almost for joy, and cry, "She's dead."
   The soldiers shout; you then perhaps may sigh
   And muster all your Roman gravity.   8
   Ventidius chides; and straight your brow clears up,
   As I had never been.

ANTONY   Gods, 'tis too much—
   Too much for man to bear.

CLEOPATRA   What is 't for me, then,   9
   A weak, forsaken woman and a lover?—

1 Here let me breathe my last. Envy me not
This minute in your arms. I'll die apace,
As fast as e'er I can, and end your trouble.

ANTONY   Die! Rather let me perish; loosened nature
Leap from its hinges! Sink the props of heaven,
2 And fall the skies to crush the nether world!
My eyes, my soul, my all! [embraces her]

VENTIDIUS   And what's this toy
In balance with your fortune, honor, fame?

ANTONY   What is 't, Ventidius? It outweighs 'em all;
3 Why, we have more than conquered Caesar now.
My queen's not only innocent, but loves me.
This, this is she who drags me down to ruin!
"But could she 'scape without me, with what haste
Would she let slip her hold and make to shore
And never look behind!"
4 Down on thy knees, blasphemer as thou art,
And ask forgiveness of wronged innocence.

VENTIDIUS   I'll rather die than take it. Will you go?

ANTONY   Go! Whither? Go from all that's excellent!
Faith, honor, virtue, all good things forbid
5 That I should go from her who sets my love
Above the price of kingdoms. Give, you gods,
Give to your boy, your Caesar,
This rattle of a globe to play withal,
This gewgaw world, and put him cheaply off.
6 I'll not be pleased with less than Cleopatra.

CLEOPATRA   She's wholly yours. My heart's so full of joy
That I shall do some wild extravagance
Of love in public, and the foolish world.
Which knows not tenderness, will think me mad.

7 VENTIDIUS   O women! women! women! all the gods
Have not such power of doing good to man
As you of doing harm. [Exit.]

ANTONY   Our men are armed.
Unbar the gate that looks to Caesar's camp.
8 I would revenge the treachery he meant me;
And long security makes conquest easy.
I'm eager to return before I go,
For all the pleasures I have known beat thick
On my remembrance.—How I long for night!
That both the sweets of mutual love may try,
9 And once triumph o'er Caesar ere we die.

[Exeunt.]

ACT THREE

[*At one door enter* CLEOPATRA, CHARMION, IRAS, *and* ALEXAS, *a* 1
train of EGYPTIANS; *at the other,* ANTONY *and* ROMANS. *The en-*
trance on both sides is prepared by music; the trumpets first
sounding on ANTONY'S *part, then answered by timbrels, and*
such, on CLEOPATRA'S. CHARMION *and* IRAS *hold a laurel wreath*
betwixt them. A dance of EGYPTIANS. *After the ceremony* CLEO-
PATRA *crowns* ANTONY.] 2

ANTONY   I thought how those white arms would fold me in,
And strain me close and melt me into love;
So pleased with that sweet image, I sprung forwards,
And added all my strength to every blow.

CLEOPATRA   Come to me, come, my soldier, to my arms! 3
You've been too long away from my embraces,
But, when I have you fast and all my own,
With broken murmurs and with amorous sighs.
I'll say you were unkind, and punish you,
And mark you red with many an eager kiss. 4

ANTONY   My brighter Venus!

CLEOPATRA   O my greater Mars!

ANTONY   Thou join'st us well, my love!
Suppose me come from the Phlegraean plains
Where gasping giants lay, cleft by my sword, 5
And mountain-tops pared off each other blow
To bury those I slew. Receive me, goddess!
Let Caesar spread his subtle nets, like Vulcan;
In thy embraces I would be beheld
By heaven and earth at once;
And make their envy what they meant their sport. 6
Let those who took us blush; I would love on
With awful state, regardless of their frowns,
As their superior god.
There's no satiety of love in thee:
Enjoyed, thou still art new; perpetual spring 7
Is in thy arms; the ripened fruit but falls,
And blossoms rise to fill its empty place,
And I grow rich by giving.

[*Enter* VENTIDIUS, *and stands apart.*]

8
ALEXAS   Oh, now the danger's past, your general comes!
He joins not in your joys, nor minds your triumphs;

31

1   But with contracted brows looks frowning on,
       As envying your success.

ANTONY   Now, on my soul, he loves me; truly loves me;
       He never flattered me in any vice,
       But awes me with his virtue. Even this minute
2   Methinks, he has a right of chiding me.—
       Lead to the temple—I'll avoid his presence;
       It checks too strong upon me.

3   [*Exeunt the rest. As* ANTONY *is going,* VENTIDIUS *pulls him by the robe.*]

VENTIDIUS   Emperor!

ANTONY [*looking back*] 'Tis the old argument. I pr'ythee, spare
       me.

VENTIDIUS   But this one hearing, emperor.

4   ANTONY   Let go
       My robe; or, by my father Hercules—

VENTIDIUS   By Hercules his father, that's yet greater,
       I bring you somewhat you would wish to know.

5   ANTONY   Thou see'st we are observed; attend me here,
       And I'll return. [*Exit.*]

VENTIDIUS   I'm waning in his favor, yet I love him;
       I love this man who runs to meet his ruin;
       And sure the gods, like me, are fond of him.
       His virtues lie so mingled with his crimes,
6   As would confound their choice to punish one
       And not reward the other.

       [*Enter* ANTONY.]

7   ANTONY   We can conquer,
       You see, without your aid.
       We have dislodged their troops;
       They look on us at distance and, like curs
       'Scaped from the lion's paw, they bay far off,
       And lick their wounds and faintly threaten war.
8   Five thousand Romans with their faces upward
       Lie breathless on the plain.

VENTIDIUS   'Tis well; and he
       Who lost them could have spared ten thousand more.
       Yet if, by this advantage, you could gain
9   An easier peace while Caesar doubts the chance
       Of arms—

ANTONY   Oh, think not on 't, Ventidius!
  The boy pursues my ruin, he'll no peace;
  His malice is considerate in advantage.
  Oh, he's the coolest murderer! so staunch,
  He kills, and keeps his temper.

VENTIDIUS   Have you no friend
  In all his army who has power to move him?
  Maecenas, or Agrippa, might do much.

ANTONY   They're both too deep in Caesar's interests.
  We'll work it out by dint of sword, or perish.

VENTIDIUS   Fain I would find some other.

ANTONY   Thank thy love.
  Some four or five such victories as this
  Will save thy further pains.

VENTIDIUS   Expect no more—Caesar is on his guard.
  I know, sir, you have conquered against odds,
  But still you draw supplies from one poor town,
  And of Egyptians. He has all the world,
  And at his back nations come pouring in
  To fill the gaps you make. Pray, think again,

ANTONY   Why dost thou drive me from myself, to search
  For foreign aids?—to hunt my memory,
  And range all o'er a waste and barren place
  To find a friend? The wretched have no friends.—
  Yet I had one, the bravest youth of Rome,
  Whom Caesar loves beyond the love of women;
  He could resolve his mind as fire does wax,
  From that hard, rugged image melt him down,
  And mold him in what softer form he pleased.

VENTIDIUS   Him would I see—that man of all the world;
  Just such a one we want.

ANTONY   He loved me, too;
  I was his soul; he lived not but in me.
  We were so closed within each other's breasts,
  The rivets were not found that joined us first.
  That does not reach us yet; we were so mixed
  As meeting streams, both to ourselves were lost;
  We were one mass; we could not give or take
  But from the same, for he was I, I he.

VENTIDIUS [aside]   He moves as I would wish him.

ANTONY   After this
  I need not tell his name.—'Twas Dolabella.

VENTIDIUS   He's now in Caesar's camp.

1 ANTONY   No matter where.
    Since he's no longer mine. He took unkindly
    That I forbade him Cleopatra's sight,
    Because I feared he loved her. He confessed
    He had a warmth which, for my sake, he stifled,
    For 'twere impossible that two, so one,
2   Should not have loved the same. When he departed,
    He took no leave, and that confirmed my thoughts.

VENTIDIUS   It argues that he loved you more than her,
    Else he had stayed. But he perceived you jealous,
    And would not grieve his friend. I know he loves you.

3 ANTONY   I should have seen him, then, ere now.

VENTIDIUS   Perhaps
    He has thus long been laboring for your peace.

ANTONY   Would he were here!

4 VENTIDIUS   Would you believe he loved you?
    I read your answer in your eyes—you would.
    Not to conceal it longer, he has sent
    A messenger from Caesar's camp with letters.

ANTONY   Let him appear.

5 VENTIDIUS   I'll bring him instantly.

[*Exit* VENTIDIUS, *re-enters immediately with* DOLABELLA.]

ANTONY   'Tis he himself! himself, by holy friendship! [*runs to em-
    brace him*]
6   Art thou returned at last, my better half?
    Come, give me all myself! Let me not live,
    If the young bridegroom, longing for his night,
    Was ever half so fond!

DOLABELLA   I must be silent, for my soul is busy
7   About a nobler work: she's new come home,
    Like a long-absent man, and wanders o'er
    Each room, a stranger to her own, to look
    If all be safe.

ANTONY   Thou hast what's left of me;
8   For I am now so sunk from what I was,
    Thou find'st me at my lowest water-mark.
    The rivers that ran in and raised my fortunes
    Are all dried up, or take another course;
    What I have left is from my native spring.
    I've still a heart that swells in scorn of fate
9   And lifts me to my banks.

DOLABELLA   Still you are lord of all the world to me.

ANTONY   Why, than I yet am so; for thou art all.
 If I had any joy when thou wert absent,
 I grudged it to myself; methought I robbed
 Thee of thy part. But, O my Dolabella!
 Thou hast beheld me other than I am.
 Hast thou not seen my morning chambers filled
 With sceptred slaves who waited to salute me?
 With eastern monarchs who forgot the sun
 To worship my uprising?—menial kings
 Ran coursing up and down my palace-yard,
 Stood silent in my presence, watched my eyes,
 And at my least command all started out
 Like racers to the goal.

DOLABELLA   Slaves to your fortune.

ANTONY   Fortune is Caesar's now; and what am I?

VENTIDIUS   What you have made yourself; I will not flatter.

ANTONY   Is this friendly done?

DOLABELLA   Yes; when his end is so, I must join with him;
 Indeed, I must; and yet you must not chide;
 Why am I else your friend?

ANTONY   Take heed, young man,
 How thou upbraid'st my love. The queen has eyes,
 And thou, too, hast a soul. Canst thou remember
 When, swelled with hatred, thou beheld'st her first,
 As accessory to thy brother's death?

DOLABELLA   Spare my remembrance; 'twas a guilty day
 And still the blush hangs here.

ANTONY   To clear herself
 For sending him no aid, she came from Egypt.
 Her galley down the silver Cydnos rowed,
 The tackling silk, the streamers waved with gold;
 The gentle winds were lodged in purple sails;
 Her nymphs, like Nereids, round her couch were placed,
 Where she, another sea-born Venus, lay.

DOLABELLA   No more; I would not hear it.

ANTONY   Oh, you must!
 She lay, and leant her cheek upon her hand,
 And cast a look so languishingly sweet
 As if, secure of all beholders' hearts,
 Neglecting, she could take them. Boys like Cupids
 Stood fanning with their painted wings the winds
 That played about her face; but if she smiled,
 A darting glory seemed to blaze abroad,

1   That men's desiring eyes were never wearied,
But hung upon the object. To soft flutes
The silver oars kept time; and while they played,
The hearing gave new pleasure to the sight,
And both, to thought. 'Twas heaven or somewhat more;
For she so charmed all hearts, that gazing crowds
2   Stood panting on the shore, and wanted breath
To give their welcome voice.
    Then, Dolabella, where was then thy soul?
Was not thy fury quite disarmed with wonder?
Didst thou not shrink behind me from those eyes
And whisper in my ear "Oh, tell her not
3   That I accused her of my brother's death?"

DOLABELLA   And should my weakness be a plea for yours?
Mine was an age when love might be excused,
When kindly warmth, and when my springing youth,
Made it a debt to nature. Yours—
4
VENTIDIUS   Speak boldly.
    Yours, he would say, in your declining age,
When no more heat was left but what you forced,
When all the sap was needful for the trunk,
When it went down, then you constrained the course,
5   And robbed from nature to supply desire;
In you (I would not use so harsh a word)
'Tis but plain dotage.

ANTONY   Ha!

DOLABELLA   'Twas urged too home.—
6   But yet the loss was private that I made;
'Twas but myself I lost. I lost no legions;
I had no world to lose, no people's love.

ANTONY   This from a friend?

DOLABELLA   Yes, Antony, a true one;
7   A friend so tender that each word I speak
Stabs my own heart before it reach your ear.
Oh, judge me not less kind because I chide!
To Caesar I excuse you.

ANTONY   O ye gods!
8   Have I then lived to be excused to Caesar?

DOLABELLA   As to your equal.

ANTONY   Well, he's but my equal;
While I wear this, he never shall be more.

9   DOLABELLA   I bring conditions from him.

ANTONY   Are they noble?

Methinks thou shouldst not bring them else; yet he   1
Is full of deep dissembling; knows no honor
Divided from his interest. Fate mistook him,
For nature meant him for an usurer;
He's fit indeed to buy, not conquer, kingdoms.

VENTIDIUS   Then, granting this,   2
   What power was theirs who wrought so hard a temper
   To honorable terms?

ANTONY   It was my Dolabella, or some god.

DOLABELLA   Nor I, nor yet Maecenas, nor Agrippa;
   They were your enemies, and I, a friend,   3
   Too weak alone; yet 'twas a Roman's deed.

ANTONY   'Twas like a Roman done; show me that man
   Who has preserved my life, my love, my honor;
   Let me but see his face.

VENTIDIUS   That task is mine,   4
   And, Heaven, thou know'st how pleasing. [*Exit* VENTIDIUS.]

DOLABELLA   You'll remember
   To whom you stand obliged?

ANTONY   When I forget it,
   Be thou unkind, and that's my greatest curse.   5
   My queen shall thank him, too.

DOLABELLA   I fear she will not.

ANTONY   But she shall do 't—the queen, my Dolabella!
   Hast thou not still some grudgings of thy fever?
                         6

DOLABELLA   I would not see her lost.

ANTONY   When I forsake her,
   Leave me, my better stars! for she has truth
   Beyond her beauty. Caesar tempted her,
   At no less price than kingdoms, to betray me,   7
   But she resisted all; and yet thou chid'st me
   For loving her too well. Could I do so?

[*Re-enter* VENTIDIUS *with* OCTAVIA, *leading* ANTONY's *two little*
   DAUGHTERS]

DOLABELLA   Yes; there's my reason.   8

ANTONY   Where?—Octavia there! [*starting back*]

VENTIDIUS   What—is she poison to you?—a disease?
   Look on her, view her well, and those she brings.
   Are they all strangers to your eyes? has nature   9
   No secret call, no whisper they are yours?

1 DOLABELLA   For shame, my lord, if not for love, receive them
With kinder eyes. If you confess a man,
Meet them, embrace them, bid them welcome to you.
Your arms should open, even without your knowledge,
To clasp them in; your feet should turn to wings,
To bear you to them; and your eyes dart out
2 And aim a kiss ere you could reach the lips.

ANTONY   I stood amazed to think how they came hither.

VENTIDIUS   I sent for 'em; I brought 'em in, unknown
To Cleopatra's guards.

3 DOLABELLA   Yet are you cold?

OCTAVIA   Thus long I have attended for my welcome,
Which, as a stranger, sure I might expect.
Who am I?

ANTONY   Caesar's sister.

4 OCTAVIA   That's unkind.
Had I been nothing more than Caesar's sister,
Know, I had still remained in Caesar's camp.
But your Octavia, your much injured wife,
Though banished from your bed, driven from your house,
5 In spite of Caesar's sister, still is yours.
'Tis true, I have a heart disdains your coldness,
And prompts me not to seek what you should offer;
But a wife's virtue still surmounts that pride.
I come to claim you as my own; to show
My duty first; to ask, nay beg, your kindness.
6 Your hand, my lord; 'tis mine, and I will have it. [taking his hand]

VENTIDIUS   Do, take it; thou deserv'st it.

DOLABELLA   On my soul,
And so she does; she's neither too submissive,
Nor yet too haughty; but so just a mean
7 Shows, as it ought, a wife and Roman too.

ANTONY   I fear, Octavia, you have begged my life.

OCTAVIA   Begged it, my lord?

ANTONY   Yes, begged it, my ambassadress;
8 Poorly and basely begged it of your brother.

OCTAVIA   Poorly and basely I could never beg.
Nor could my brother grant.

ANTONY   Shall I, who, to my kneeling slave, could say,
"Rise up and be a king," shall I fall down
9 And cry, "Forgive me, Caesar?" Shall I set
A man, my equal, in the place of Jove,

As he could give me being? No—that word
"Forgive" would choke me up
And die upon my tongue.

DOLABELLA   You shall not need it.

ANTONY   I will not need it. Come, you've all betrayed me—
My friend too!—to receive some vile conditions.
My wife has bought me with her prayers and tears,
And now I must become her branded slave.
In every peevish mood she will upbraid
The life she gave; if I but look awry,
She cries, "I'll tell my brother."

OCTAVIA   My hard fortune
Subjects me still to your unkind mistakes.
But the conditions I have brought are such
You need not blush to take; I love your honor,
Because 'tis mine. It never shall be said
Octavia's husband was her brother's slave.
Sir, you are free—free, even from her you loathe;
For, though my brother bargains for your love,
Makes me the price and cément of your peace,
I have a soul like yours; I cannot take
Your love as alms, nor beg what I deserve.
I'll tell my brother we are reconciled;
He shall draw back his troops, and you shall march
To rule the East. I may be dropped at Athens—
No matter where. I never will complain,
But only keep the barren name of wife,
And rid you of the trouble.

VENTIDIUS   Was ever such a strife of sullen honor!
Both scorn to be obliged.

DOLABELLA   Oh, she has touched him in the tenderest part;
See how he reddens with despite and shame,
To be outdone in generosity!

VENTIDIUS   See how he winks! how he dries up a tear,
That fain would fall!

ANTONY   Octavia, I have heard you, and must praise
The greatness of your soul;
But cannot yield to what you have proposed,
For I can ne'er be conquered but by love,
And you do all for duty. You would free me,
And would be dropped at Athens; was 't not so?

OCTAVIA   It was, my lord.

ANTONY   Then I must be obliged
To one who loves me not; who, to herself,

1 May call me thankless and ungrateful man.—
   I'll not endure it—no.

VENTIDIUS [*aside*] I am glad it pinches there.

OCTAVIA Would you triumph o'er poor Octavia's virtue?
   That pride was all I had to bear me up;
2 That you might think you owed me for your life,
   And owed it to my duty, not my love.
   I have been injured, and my haughty soul
   Could brook but ill the man who slights my bed.

ANTONY Therefore you love me not.

3 OCTAVIA   Therefore, my lord,
   I should not love you.

ANTONY Therefore you would leave me?

OCTAVIA And therefore I should leave you—if I could.

4 DOLABELLA Her soul's too great, after such injuries,
   To say she loves; and yet she lets you see it.
   Her modesty and silence plead her cause.

ANTONY O Dolabella, which way shall I turn?
   I find a secret yielding in my soul;
5 But Cleopatra, who would die with me,
   Must she be left? Pity pleads for Octavia,
   But does it not plead more for Cleopatra?

VENTIDIUS Justice and pity both plead for Octavia;
   For Cleopatra, neither.
   One would be ruined with you, but she first
6 Had ruined you; the other, you have ruined,
   And yet she would preserve you.
   In everything their merits are unequal.

ANTONY O my distracted soul!

OCTAVIA Sweet Heaven, compose it!—
7 Come, come, my lord, if I can pardon you,
   Methinks you should accept it. Look on these—
   Are they not yours? or stand they thus neglected
   As they are mine? Go to him, children, go;
   Kneel to him, take him by the hand, speak to him,
8 For you may speak and he may own you, too,
   Without a blush—and so he cannot all
   His children. Go, I say, and pull him to me,
   And pull him to yourselves from that bad woman.
   You, Agrippina, hang upon his arms,
   And you, Antonia, clasp about his waist.
9 If he will shake you off, if he will dash you

Against the pavement, you must bear it, children,   1
For you are mine, and I was born to suffer.

[*Here the* CHILDREN *go to him, et cetera.*]

VENTIDIUS   Was ever sight so moving?—Emperor!

DOLABELLA   Friend!   2

OCTAVIA   Husband!

BOTH CHILDREN   Father!

ANTONY   I am vanquished. Take me,
    Octavia—take me, children—share me all. [*embracing them*]   3
    I've been a thriftless debtor to your loves,
    And run out much, in riot, from your stock,
    But all shall be amended.

OCTAVIA   O blest hour!

DOLABELLA   O happy change!   4

VENTIDIUS   My joy stops at my tongue,
    But it has found two channels here for one,
    And bubbles out above.

ANTONY [*to* OCTAVIA]   This is thy triumph. Lead me where thou
    wilt,   5
    Even to thy brother's camp.

OCTAVIA   All there are yours.

[*Enter* ALEXAS *hastily.*]

ALEXAS   The queen, my mistress, sir, and yours—   6

ANTONY   'Tis past.—
    Octavia, you shall stay this night. Tomorrow
    Caesar and we are one.

[*Exit, leading* OCTAVIA; DOLABELLA *and the* CHILDREN *follow.*]   7

VENTIDIUS   There's news for you! Run, my officious eunuch,
    Be sure to be the first—haste forward!
    Haste, my dear eunuch, haste! [*Exit.*]

ALEXAS   This downright fighting fool, this thick-skulled hero,   8
    This blunt, unthinking instrument of death,
    With plain, dull virtue has outgone my wit.
    Pleasure forsook my earliest infancy;
    The luxury of others robbed my cradle,
    And ravished thence the promise of a man.
    Cast out from nature, disinherited   9

Of what her meanest children claim by kind,
Yet greatness kept me from contempt. That's gone.
Had Cleopatra followed my advice,
Then he had been betrayed who now forsakes.
She dies for love, but she has known its joys.
Gods, is this just that I, who know no joys,
Must die because she loves?

[*Enter* CLEOPATRA, CHARMION, IRAS, *train*.]

O madam, I have seen what blasts my eyes!
Octavia's here.

CLEOPATRA   Peace with that raven's note.
I know it, too, and now am in
The pangs of death.

ALEXAS   You are no more a queen—
Egypt is lost.

CLEOPATRA   What tell'st thou me of Egypt?
My life, my soul is lost! Octavia has him!—
O fatal name to Cleopatra's love!
My kisses, my embraces now are hers,
While I—But thou hast seen my rival. Speak—
Does she deserve this blessing? Is she fair?
Bright as a goddess? and is all perfection
Confined to her?—It is. Poor I was made
Of that coarse matter which, when she was finished,
The gods threw by for rubbish.

ALEXAS   She's indeed a very miracle.

CLEOPATRA   Death to my hopes, a miracle!

ALEXAS [*bowing*]   A miracle—
I mean, of goodness; for in beauty, madam,
You make all wonders cease.

CLEOPATRA   I was too rash.
Take this in part of recompense. But, oh! [*giving a ring*]
I fear thou flatter'st me.

CHARMION   She comes! She's here!

IRAS   Fly, madam, Caesar's sister!

CLEOPATRA   Were she the sister of the thunderer Jove,
And bore her brother's lightning in her eye,
Thus would I face my rival.

[*Meets* OCTAVIA *with* VENTIDIUS. OCTAVIA *bears up to her. Their
trains come up on either side.*]

OCTAVIA   I need not ask if you are Cleopatra,
  Your haughty carriage—   1

CLEOPATRA   Shows I am a queen.
  Nor need I ask you who you are.

OCTAVIA   A Roman;
  A name that makes and can unmake a queen.   2

CLEOPATRA   Your lord, the man who serves me, is a Roman.

OCTAVIA   He was a Roman, till he lost that name
  To be a slave in Egypt; but I come
  To free him thence.
                                                             3
CLEOPATRA   Peace, peace, my lover's Juno.
  When he grew weary of that household clog,
  He chose my easier bonds.

OCTAVIA   I wonder not
  Your bonds are easy. You have long been practiced
  In that lascivious art. He's not the first   4
  For whom you spread your snares: let Caesar witness.

CLEOPATRA   I loved not Caesar; 'twas but gratitude
  I paid his love. The worst your malice can
  Is but to say the greatest of mankind
  Has been my slave. The next, but far above him   5
  In my esteem, is he whom law calls yours,
  But whom his love made mine.

OCTAVIA [*coming up closer to her*]   I would view nearer
  That face which has so long usurped my right,
  To find the inevitable charms that catch   6
  Mankind so sure, that ruined my dear lord.

CLEOPATRA   Oh, you do well to search, for had you known
  But half these charms, you had not lost his heart.

OCTAVIA   Far be their knowledge from a Roman lady—
  Far from a modest wife! Shame of our sex,   7
  Dost thou not blush to own those black endearments
  That make sin pleasing?

CLEOPATRA   You may blush, who want them.
  If bounteous nature, if indulgent heaven
  Have given me charms to please the bravest man,   8
  Should I not thank them? Should I be ashamed,
  And not be proud? I am, that he has loved me.
  And when I love not him, heaven change this face
  For one like that.

OCTAVIA   Thou lov'st him not so well.   9

CLEOPATRA   I love him better, and deserve him more.

OCTAVIA   You do not—cannot. You have been his ruin.
Who made him cheap at Rome but Cleopatra?
Who made him scorned abroad but Cleopatra?
At Actium, who betrayed him? Cleopatra!
Who made his children orphans, and poor me
A wretched widow? Only Cleopatra.

CLEOPATRA   Yet she who loves him best is Cleopatra.
If you have suffered, I have suffered more.
You bear the specious title of a wife
To gild your cause and draw the pitying world
To favor it. The world contemns poor me,
For I have lost my honor, lost my fame,
And stained the glory of my royal house,
And all to bear the branded name of mistress.
There wants but life, and that, too, I would lose
For him I love.

OCTAVIA   Be 't so, then; take thy wish.

[*Exit followed by her train.*]

CLEOPATRA   And 'tis my wish,
Now he is lost for whom alone I lived.
My sight grows dim, and every object dances
And swims before me in the maze of death.
My spirits, while they were opposed, kept up;
They could not sink beneath a rival's scorn,
But now she's gone, they faint.

ALEXAS   Mine have had leisure
To recollect their strength and furnish counsel
To ruin her, who else must ruin you.

CLEOPATRA   Vain promiser!
Lead me, my Charmion; nay, your hand, too, Iras.
My grief has weight enough to sink you both.
Conduct me to some solitary chamber,
And draw the curtains round;
Then leave me to myself, to take alone
My fill of grief.
There I till death will his unkindness weep,
As harmless infants moan themselves asleep.

[*Exeunt.*]

ACT FOUR

[ANTONY, DOLABELLA.]   1

DOLABELLA Why would you shift it from yourself on me?
  Can you not tell her you must part?

ANTONY   I cannot.
  I could pull out an eye and bid it go,
  And t' other should not weep. O Dolabella,   2
  How many deaths are in this word, *Depart!*
  I dare not trust my tongue to tell her so—
  One look of hers would thaw me into tears,
  And I should melt till I were lost again.

DOLABELLA Then let Ventidius—
  He's rough by nature.   3

ANTONY Oh, he'll speak too harshly;
  He'll kill her with the news. Thou, only thou!

DOLABELLA Nature has cast me in so soft a mould
  That but to hear a story feigned for pleasure,   4
  Of some sad lover's death moistens my eyes,
  And robs me of my manhood. I should speak
  So faintly, with such fear to grieve her heart,
  She'd not believe it earnest.

ANTONY   Therefore—therefore
  Thou, only thou art fit. Think thyself me,   5
  And when thou speak'st (but let it first be long),
  Take off the edge from every sharper sound,
  And let our parting be as gently made
  As other loves begin. Wilt thou do this?

DOLABELLA What you have said so sinks into my soul   6
  That, if I must speak, I shall speak just so.

ANTONY I leave you then to your sad task.
  Farewell!
  I sent her word to meet you. [*goes to the door and come back*]
  I forgot.   7
  Let her be told I'll make her peace with mine.
  Her crown and dignity shall be preserved,
  If I have power with Caesar.—Oh, be sure
  To think on that!

DOLABELLA   Fear not, I will remember.   8

45

1   [ANTONY *goes again to the door and comes back.*]

ANTONY   And tell her, too, how much I was constrained;
    I did not this but with extremest force.
    Desire her not to hate my memory,
    For I still cherish hers;—insist on that.

2   DOLABELLA   Trust me, I'll not forget it.

ANTONY   Then that's all. [*goes out
    and returns again*]
    Wilt thou forgive my fondness this once more?
    Tell her, though we shall never meet again,
3   If I should hear she took another love,
    The news would break my heart.—Now I must go,
    For every time I have returned, I feel
    My soul more tender, and my next command
    Would be to bid her stay, and ruin both. [*Exit.*]

4   DOLABELLA   Men are but children of a larger growth;
    Our appetites as apt to change as theirs,
    And full as craving, too, and full as vain;
    And yet the soul, shut up in her dark room,
    Viewing so clear abroad, at home sees nothing;
    But like a mole in earth, busy and blind,
5   Works all her folly up and casts it outward
    To the world's open view. Thus I discovered,
    And blamed, the love of ruined Antony,
    Yet wish that I were he, to be so ruined.

[*Enter* VENTIDIUS *above.*]

6   VENTIDIUS   Alone, and talking to himself? concerned, too?
    Perhaps my guess is right; he loved her once,
    And may pursue it still.

DOLABELLA   O friendship! friendship!
    Ill canst thou answer this; and reason, worse.
7   Unfaithful in the attempt; hopeless to win;
    And, if I win, undone; mere madness all.
    And yet the occasion's fair. What injury
    To him, to wear the robe which he throws by?

VENTIDIUS   None, none at all. This happens as I wish,
8   To ruin her yet more with Antony

[*Enter* CLEOPATRA, *talking with* ALEXAS; CHARMION, IRAS *on the
other side.*]

DOLABELLA   She comes! What charms have sorrow on that face!
    Sorrow seems pleased to dwell with so much sweetness;
9   Yet, now and then, a melancholy smile

Breaks loose like lightning in a winter's night,   1
And shows a moment's day.

VENTIDIUS   If she should love him, too—her eunuch there!
That porc'pisce bodes ill weather. Draw, draw nearer,
Sweet devil, that I may hear.

ALEXAS   Believe me; try   2

[DOLABELLA *goes over to* CHARMION *and* IRAS; *seems to talk with*
them]

To make him jealous; jealousy is like
A polished glass held to the lips when life's in doubt;   3
If there be breath, 'twill catch the damp, and show it.

CLEOPATRA   I grant you, jealousy's a proof of love,
But 'tis a weak and unavailing medicine;
It puts out the disease, and makes it show,
But has no power to cure.   4

ALEXAS   'Tis your last remedy, and strongest, too.
And then this Dolabella—who so fit
To practice on? He's handsome, valiant, young,
And looks as he were laid for nature's bait
To catch weak women's eyes.   5
He stands already more than half suspected
Of loving you. The least kind word or glance
You give this youth will kindle him with love;
Then, like a burning vessel set adrift,
You'll send him down amain before the wind
To fire the heart of jealous Antony.   6

CLEOPATRA   Can I do this? Ah, no. My love's so true
That I can neither hide it where it is,
Nor show it where it is not. Nature meant me
A wife—a silly, harmless, household dove,
Fond without art, and kind without deceit;   7
But Fortune, that has made a mistress of me,
Has thrust me out to the wide world, unfurnished
Of falsehood to be happy.

ALEXAS   Force yourself.
The event will be, your lover will return   8
Doubly desirous to possess the good
Which once he feared to lose.

CLEOPATRA   I must attempt it,

[*Exit* ALEXAS.]
                                                                                9

1   But oh, with what regret! [*She comes up to* DOLABELLA.]

VENTIDIUS   So, now the scene draws near; they're in my reach.

CLEOPATRA [*to* DOLABELLA]   Discoursing with my women! Might
    not I
    Share in your entertainment?

2
CHARMION   You have been
    The subject of it, madam.

CLEOPATRA   How! and how?

IRAS   Such praises of your beauty!

3 CLEOPATRA   Mere poetry.
    Your Roman wits, your Gallus and Tibullus;
    Have taught you this from Cytheris and Delia.

DOLABELLA   Those Roman wits have never been in Egypt;
    Cytheris and Delia else had been unsung.
4   I, who have seen—had I been born a poet,
    Should choose a nobler name.

CLEOPATRA   You flatter me.
    But 'tis your nation's vice. All of your country
    Are flatterers, and all false. Your friend's like you.
    I'm sure he sent you not to speak these words.
5
DOLABELLA   No, madam, yet he sent me—

CLEOPATRA   Well, he sent you—

DOLABELLA   Of a less pleasing errand.

CLEOPATRA   How less pleasing?
6   Less to yourself, or me?

DOLABELLA   Madam, to both.
    For you must mourn, and I must grieve to cause it.

CLEOPATRA   You, Charmion, and your fellow, stand at distance—
7   [*Aside*] Hold up, my spirits.—Well, now your mournful matter,
    For I'm prepared—perhaps can guess it, too.

DOLABELLA   I wish you would, for 'tis a thankless office
    To tell ill news; and I, of all your sex,
    Most fear displeasing you.

8 CLEOPATRA   Of all your sex
    I soonest could forgive you if you should.

VENTIDIUS   Most delicate advances!—Woman! woman!
    Dear, damned, inconstant sex!

CLEOPATRA   In the first place,
9   I am to be forsaken. Is 't not so?

DOLABELLA   I wish I could not answer to that question.   1

CLEOPATRA   Then pass it o'er, because it troubles you;
I should have been more grieved another time.
Next, I'm to lose my kingdom—Farewell, Egypt!
Yet, is there any more?

DOLABELLA   Madam, I fear   2
Your too deep sense of grief has turned your reason.

CLEOPATRA   No, no, I'm not run mad; I can bear fortune,
And love may be expelled by other love,
As poisons are by poisons.

DOLABELLA   You o'erjoy me, madam,   3
To find your griefs so moderately borne.
You've heard the worst; all are not false like him.

CLEOPATRA   No. Heaven forbid they should.

DOLABELLA   Some men are
constant.   4

CLEOPATRA   And constancy deserves reward, that's certain.

DOLABELLA   Deserves it not, but give it leave to hope.

VENTIDIUS   I'll swear thou hast my leave. I have enough.—
But how to manage this! Well, I'll consider. [*Exit.*]   5

DOLABELLA   I came prepared
To tell you heavy news—news which, I thought,
Would fright the blood from your pale cheeks to hear,
But you have met it with a cheerfulness
That makes my task more easy; and my tongue,   6
Which on another's message was employed,
Would gladly speak its own.

CLEOPATRA   Hold, Dolobella.
First tell me, were you chosen by my lord?
Or sought you this employment?   7

DOLABELLA   He picked me out; and, as his bosom friend,
He charged me with his words.

CLEOPATRA   The message then
I know was tender, and each accent smooth,
To mollify that rugged word, *Depart*.   8

DOLABELLA   Oh, you mistake. He chose the harshest words;
With fiery eyes and with contracted brows
He coined his face in the severest stamp;
And fury shook his fabric like an earthquake;
He heaved for vent, and burst like bellowing Aetna.
In sounds scarce human—"Hence, away, for ever,   9

1   Let her begone, the blot of my renown,
       And bane of all my hopes!

       [*All the time of this speech* CLEOPATRA *seems more and more con-
       cerned till she sinks quite down.*]

2   Let her be driven as far as man can think
       From man's commèrce! she'll poison to the center."

CLEOPATRA   Oh, I can bear no more!

DOLABELLA   Help, help!—O wretch! O cursèd, cursèd wretch!
       What have I done!

3   CHARMION   Help, chafe her temples, Iras.

IRAS   Bend, bend her forward quickly.

CHARMION   Heaven be praised,
       She comes again.

4   CLEOPATRA   Oh, let him not approach me.
       Why have you brought me back to this loathed being,
       The abode of falsehood, violated vows,
       And injured love? For pity, let me go;
       For, if there be a place of long repose,
       I'm sure I want it. My disdainful lord
5   Can never break that quiet, nor awake
       The sleeping soul with hollowing in my tomb
       Such words as fright her hence.—Unkind, unkind!

DOLABELLA [*kneeling*]   Believe me, 'tis against myself I speak.
       That sure deserves belief—I injured him:
6   My friend ne'er spoke those words. Oh, had you seen
       How often he came back, and every time
       With something more obliging and more kind
       To add to what he said; what dear farewells;
       How almost vanquished by his love he parted,
       And leaned to what unwillingly he left!
7   I, traitor as I was, for love of you
       (But what can you not do, who made me false?)
       I forged that lie; for whose forgiveness kneels
       This self-accused, self-punished criminal.

CLEOPATRA   With how much ease believe we what we wish!
       Rise, Dolabella; if you have been guilty,
8   I have contributed, and too much love
       Has made me guilty too.
       The advance of kindness which I made was feigned
       To call back fleeting love by jealousy,
       But 'twould not last. Oh, rather let me lose
9   Than so ignobly trifle with his heart!

DOLABELLA   I find your breast fenced round from human reach,   1
   Transparent as a rock of solid crystal,
   Seen through, but never pierced. My friend, my friend!
   What endless treasure hast thou thrown away,
   And scattered, like an infant, in the ocean,
   Vain sums of wealth, which none can gather thence!
                                                   2

CLEOPATRA   Could you not beg
   An hour's admittance to his private ear?
   Like one who wanders through long barren wilds,
   And yet foreknows no hospitable inn
   Is near to succor hunger, eats his fill
   Before his painful march,
   So would I feed a while my famished eyes
   Before we part, for I have far to go,
   If death be far, and never must return.
                                                   3

[*Enter* VENTIDIUS *with* OCTAVIA, *behind.*]

VENTIDIUS   From hence you may discover—Oh, sweet, sweet!   4
   Would you, indeed? The pretty hand in earnest?

DOLABELLA   I will, for this reward. [*Takes her hand*] Draw it not
   back,
   'Tis all I e'er will beg.

VENTIDIUS   They turn upon us.   5

OCTAVIA   What quick eyes has guilt!

VENTIDIUS   Seem not to have observed them, and go on.

[*They enter.*]
                                                   6

DOLABELLA   Saw you the the emperor, Ventidius?

VENTIDIUS   No.
   I sought him, but I heard that he was private,
   None with him but Hipparchus, his freedman.

DOLABELLA   Know you his business?
                                                   7

VENTIDIUS   Giving him instructions
   And letters to his brother Caesar.

DOLABELLA   Well,
   He must be found.

[*Exeunt* DOLABELLA *and* CLEOPATRA.]
                                                 8

OCTAVIA   Most glorious impudence!

VENTIDIUS   She looked, methought,
   As she would say, "Take your old man, Octavia,
   Thank you, I'm better here." Well, but what use
   Make we of this discovery?
                                                   9

1 OCTAVIA   Let it die.

VENTIDIUS   I pity Dolabella. But she's dangerous;
    Her eyes have power beyond Thessalian charms
    To draw the moon from heaven; for eloquence,
    The sea-green Syrens taught her voice their flatt'ry;
2   And while she speaks, night steals upon the day,
    Unmarked of those that hear. Then she's so charming
    Age buds at sight of her, and swells to youth;
    The holy priests gaze on her when she smiles,
    And with heaved hands, forgetting gravity,
    They bless her wanton eyes. Even I, who hate her,
3   With a malignant joy behold such beauty,
    And while I curse, desire it. Antony
    Must needs have some remains of passion still,
    Which may ferment into a worse relapse
    It now not fully cured. I know, this minute,
4   With Caesar he's endeavoring her peace.

OCTAVIA   You have prevailed:—But for a further purpose
        [*walks off*]
    I'll prove how he will relish this discovery.
    What, make a strumpet's peace! it swells my heart;
    It must not, shall not be.

5 VENTIDIUS   His guards appear.
    Let me begin, and you shall second me.

[*Enter* ANTONY.]

ANTONY   Octavia, I was looking you, my love.
6   What, are your letters ready? I have given
    My last instructions.

OCTAVIA   Mine, my lord, are written.

ANTONY   Ventidius. [*drawing him aside*]

7 VENTIDIUS   My lord?

ANTONY   A word in private.—
    When saw you Dolabella?

VENTIDIUS   Now, my lord,
    He parted hence; and Cleopatra with him.

8 ANTONY   Speak softly.—'Twas by my command he went
    To bear my last farewell.

VENTIDIUS [*aloud*]   It looked indeed
    Like your farewell.

9 ANTONY   More softly.—My farewell?

What secret meaning have you in those words 1
Of "my farewell?" He did it by my order.

VENTIDIUS [*aloud*] Then he obeyed your order. I suppose
You bid him do it with all gentleness,
All kindness, and all—love.

ANTONY   How she mourned, 2
The poor forsaken creature!

VENTIDIUS She took it as she ought; she bore your parting
As she did Caesar's, as she would another's,
Were a new love to come.

ANTONY [*aloud*]   Thou dost belie her; 3
Most basely and maliciously belie her.

VENTIDIUS I thought not to displease you; I have done.

OCTAVIA [*coming up*] You seem disturbed, my lord.

ANTONY   A very trifle. 4
Retire, my love.

VENTIDIUS   It was indeed a trifle.
He sent—

ANTONY [*angrily*] No more. Look how thou disobey'st me;
Thy life shall answer it. 5

OCTAVIA   Then 'tis no trifle.

VENTIDIUS [*to* OCTAVIA] 'Tis less—a very nothing. You too saw it,
As well as I, and therefore 'tis no secret.

ANTONY She saw it!
6
VENTIDIUS   Yes. She saw young Dolabella—

ANTONY Young Dolabella!

VENTIDIUS   Young, I think him young,
And handsome too, and so do others think him.
But what of that? He went by your command, 7
Indeed, 'tis probable, with some kind message,
For she received it graciously; she smiled;
And then he grew familiar with her hand,
Squeezed it, and worried it with ravenous kisses;
She blushed, and sighed, and smiled, and blushed again;
At last she took occasion to talk softly, 8
And brought her cheek up close, and leaned on his;
At which, he whispered kisses back on hers;
And then she cried aloud that constancy
Should be rewarded.

OCTAVIA   This I saw and heard. 9

1   ANTONY   What woman was it whom you heard and saw
So playful with my friend? Not Cleopatra?

VENTIDIUS   Even she, my lord,

ANTONY   My Cleopatra?

2   VENTIDIUS   Your Cleopatra;
Dolabella's Cleopatra;
Every man's Cleopatra.

ANTONY   Thou liest.

VENTIDIUS   I do not lie, my lord.
3   Is this so strange? Should mistresses be left,
And not provide against a time of change?
You know she's not much used to lonely nights.

ANTONY   I'll think no more on 't.
I know 'tis false, and see the plot betwixt you.—
You needed not have gone this way, Octavia.
4   What harms it you that Cleopatra's just?
She's mine no more. I see, and I forgive.
Urge it no further, love.

OCTAVIA   Are you concerned
That she's found false?

5   ANTONY   I should be, were it so,
For though 'tis past, I would not that the world
Should tax my former choice, that I loved one
Of so light note, but I forgive you both.

VENTIDIUS   What has my age deserved that you should think
6   I would abuse your ears with perjury?
If Heaven be true, she's false.

ANTONY   Though heaven and earth
Should witness it, I'll not believe her tainted.

VENTIDIUS   I'll bring you, then, a witness
7   From hell to prove her so.—Nay, go not back,

[*seeing* ALEXAS *just entering, and starting back*]

For stay you must and shall.

ALEXAS   What means my lord?

8   VENTIDIUS   To make you do what most you hate,—speak truth.
You are of Cleopatra's private counsel,
Of her bed-counsel, her lascivious hours;
Are conscious of each nightly change she makes,
And watch her, as Chaldaeans do the moon,
9   Can tell what signs she passes through, what day.

ALEXAS My noble lord!   1

VENTIDIUS   My most illustrious pander,
  No fine set speech, no cadence, no turned periods,
  But a plain homespun truth is what I ask:
  I did myself o'erhear your queen make love
  To Dolabella. Speak. For I will know   2
  By your confession what more passed betwixt them;
  How near the business draws to your employment;
  And when the happy hour.

ANTONY Speak truth, Alexas; whether it offend
  Or please Ventidius, care not. Justify
  Thy injured queen from malice. Dare his worst.   3

OCTAVIA [aside] See how he gives him courage! how he fears
  To find her false! and shuts his eyes to truth,
  Willing to be misled!

ALEXAS As far as love may plead for woman's frailty,   4
  Urged by desert and greatness of the lover,
  So far, divine Octavia, may my queen
  Stand even excused to you for loving him
  Who is your lord; so far, from brave Ventidius,
  May her past actions hope a fair report.

ANTONY 'Tis well, and truly spoken. Mark, Ventidius.   5

ALEXAS To you, most noble emperor, her strong passion
  Stands not excused, but wholly justified.
  Her beauty's charms alone, without her crown,
  From Ind and Meroë drew the distant vows
  Of sighing kings; and at her feet were laid   6
  The sceptres of the earth exposed on heaps,
  To choose where she would reign.
  She thought a Roman only could deserve her,
  And of all Romans only Antony;
  And, to be less than wife to you, disdained   7
  Their lawful passion.

ANTONY   'Tis but truth.

ALEXAS And yet, though love and your unmatched desert
  Have drawn her from the due regard of honor,
  At last Heaven opened her unwilling eyes
  To see the wrongs she offered fair Octavia,   8
  Whose holy bed she lawlessly usurped.
  The sad effects of this improsperous war
  Confirmed those pious thoughts.

VENTIDIUS [aside]   Oh, wheel you there?
  Observe him now; the man begins to mend,   9

And talk substantial reason.—Fear not, eunuch,
The emperor has given thee leave to speak.

ALEXAS   Else had I never dared to offend his ears
With what the last necessity has urged
On my forsaken mistress; yet I must not
Presume to say her heart is wholly altered.

ANTONY   No, dare not for thy life, I charge thee dare not
Pronounce that fatal word!

OCTAVIA [*aside*]   Must I bear this? Good Heaven, afford me patience!

VENTIDIUS   On, sweet eunuch; my dear half-man, proceed.

ALEXAS   Yet Dolabella
Has loved her long. He, next my god-like lord,
Deserves her best; and should she meet his passion,
Rejected as she is by him she loved—

ANTONY   Hence from my sight! for I can bear no more.
Let furies drag thee quick to hell; let all
The longer damned have rest; each torturing hand
Do thou employ till Cleopatra comes;
Then join thou too, and help to torture her!

[*Exit* ALEXAS, *thrust out by* ANTONY.]

OCTAVIA   'Tis not well,
Indeed, my lord, 'tis much unkind to me,
To show this passion, this extreme concernment
For an abandoned, faithless prostitute.

ANTONY   Octavia, leave me. I am much disordered.
Leave me, I say.

OCTAVIA   My lord!

ANTONY   I bid you leave me.

VENTIDIUS   Obey him, madam. Best withdraw a while,
And see how this will work.

OCTAVIA   Wherein have I offended you, my lord,
That I am bid to leave you? Am I false
Or infamous? Am I a Cleopatra?
Were I she,
Base as she is, you would not bid me leave you,
But hang upon my neck, take slight excuses,
And fawn upon my falsehood.

ANTONY   'Tis too much,
Too much, Octavia. I am pressed with sorrows
Too heavy to be borne, and you add more.
I would retire and recollect what's left

Of man within, to aid me.   1

OCTAVIA   You would mourn
In private for your love, who has betrayed you.
You did but half return to me; your kindness
Lingered behind with her. I hear, my lord,
You make conditions for her,   2
And would include her treaty. Wondrous proofs
Of love to me!

ANTONY   Are you my friend, Ventidius?
Or are you turned a Dolabella too,
And let this Fury loose?   3

VENTIDIUS   Oh, be advised,
Sweet madam, and retire.

OCTAVIA   Yes, I will go, but never to return.
You shall no more be haunted with this Fury.
My lord, my lord, love will not always last
When urged with long unkindness and disdain.   4
Take her again whom you prefer to me;
She stays but to be called. Poor cozened man!
Let a feigned parting give her back your heart,
Which a feigned love first got; for injured me,
Though my just sense of wrongs forbid my stay,   5
My duty shall be yours.
To the dear pledges of our former love
My tenderness and care shall be transferred,
And they shall cheer, by turns, my widowed nights.
So, take my last farewell, for I despair   6
To have you whole, and scorn to take you half.

[*Exit* OCTAVIA.]

VENTIDIUS   I combat Heaven, which blasts my best designs;
My last attempt must be to win her back;
But oh! I fear in vain. [*Exit.*]   7

ANTONY   Why was I framed with this plain, honest heart,
Which knows not to disguise its griefs and weakness,
But bears its workings outward to the world?
I should have kept the mighty anguish in,
And forced a smile at Cleopatra's falsehood.
Octavia had believed it, and had stayed.   8
But I am made a shallow-forded stream,
Seen to the bottom; all my clearness scorned,
And all my faults exposed.—See where he comes

[*Enter* DOLABELLA.]   9

Who has profaned the sacred name of friend,

1
And worn it into vileness!
With how secure a brow, and specious form,
He gilds the secret villain! Sure that face
Was meant for honesty, but Heaven mismatched it,
And furnished treason out with nature's pomp
To make its work more easy.

2
DOLABELLA   O my friend!

ANTONY   Well, Dolabella, you performed my message!

DOLABELLA   I did, unwillingly.

ANTONY   Unwillingly?
3
Was it so hard for you to bear our parting?
You should have wished it.

DOLABELLA   Why?

ANTONY   Because you love me.
And she received my message with as true,
4
With as unfeigned a sorrow as you brought it?

DOLABELLA   She loves you, even to madness.

ANTONY   Oh, I know it.
You, Dolabella, do not better know
How much she loves me. And should I
5
Forsake this beauty? This all-perfect creature?

DOLABELLA   I could not, were she mine.

ANTONY   And yet you first
Persuaded me. How come you altered since?

6
DOLABELLA   I said at first I was not fit to go;
I could not hear her sighs and see her tears,
But pity must prevail. And so perhaps
It may again with you, for I have promised
That she should take her last farewell. And see,
She comes to claim my word.

7
[Enter CLEOPATRA.]

ANTONY   False Dolabella!

DOLABELLA   What's false, my lord?

ANTONY   Why, Dolabella's false,
8
And Cleopatra's false—both false and faithless.
Draw near, you well-joined wickedness, you serpents
Whom I have in my kindly bosom warmed,
Till I am stung to death.

DOLABELLA   My lord, have I
9
Deserved to be thus used?

CLEOPATRA   Can Heaven prepare   1
    A newer torment? Can it find a curse
    Beyond our separation?

ANTONY   Yes, if fate
    Be just, much greater. Heaven should be ingenious
    In punishing such crimes. The rolling stone   2
    And gnawing vulture were slight pains, invented
    When Jove was young, and no examples known
    Of mighty ills. But you have ripened sin
    To such a monstrous growth 'twill pose the gods
    To find an equal torture. Two, two such!—
    Oh, there's no farther name,—two such! to me,   3
    To me, who locked my soul within your breasts,
    Had no desires, no joys, no life, but you.
    When half the globe was mine, I gave it you
    In dowry with my heart; I had no use,
    No fruit of all, but you. A friend and mistress
    Was what the world could give. O Cleopatra!   4
    O Dolabella! how could you betray
    This tender heart which with an infant fondness
    Lay lulled betwixt your bosoms and there slept,
    Secure of injured faith?

DOLABELLA   If she has wronged you,   5
    Heaven, hell, and you, revenge it.

ANTONY   If she wronged me!
    Thou wouldst evade thy part of guilt. But swear
    Thou lov'st not her.

DOLABELLA   Not so as I love you.   6

ANTONY   Not so? Swear, swear, I say, thou dost not love her.

DOLABELLA   No more than friendship will allow.

ANTONY   No more?
    Friendship allows thee nothing. Thou art perjured—   7
    And yet thou didst not swear thou lov'd'st her not,
    But not so much, no more. O trifling hypocrite,
    Who dar'st not own to her, thou dost not love,
    Nor own to me, thou dost. Ventidius heard it;
    Octavia saw it.

CLEOPATRA   They are enemies.   8

ANTONY   Alexas is not so. He, he confessed it;
    He, who, next hell, best knew it, he avowed it.
    Why do I seek a proof beyond yourself?
    [to DOLABELLA] You, whom I sent to bear my last farewell,
    Returned to plead her stay.   9

1 DOLABELLA   What shall I answer?
    If to have loved be guilt, then I have sinned;
    But if to have repented of that love
    Can wash away my crime, I have repented.
    Yet, if I have offended past forgiveness,
    Let not her suffer. She is innocent.
2
    CLEOPATRA   Ah, what will not a woman do who loves?
    What means will she refuse to keep that heart
    Where all her joys are placed? 'Twas I encouraged,
    'Twas I blew up the fire that scorched his soul,
    To make you jealous, and by that regain you.
3   But all in vain. I could not counterfeit;
    In spite of all the dams, my love broke o'er,
    And drowned my heart again; fate took the occasion,
    And thus one minute's feigning has destroyed
    My whole life's truth.

4   ANTONY   Thin cobweb arts of falsehood,
    Seen, and broke through at first.

    DOLABELLA   Forgive your mistress.

    CLEOPATRA   Forgive your friend.

    ANTONY   You have convinced yourselves.
5   You plead each other's cause. What witness have you
    That you but meant to raise my jealousy?

    CLEOPATRA   Ourselves, and Heaven.

    ANTONY   Guilt witnesses for guilt. Hence, love and friendship!
6   You have no longer place in human breasts;
    These two have driven you out. Avoid my sight!
    I would not kill the man whom I have loved,
    And cannot hurt the woman. But avoid me,
    I do not know how long I can be tame,
    For, if I stay one minute more, to think
7   How I am wronged, my justice and revenge
    Will cry so loud within me that my pity
    Will not be heard for either.

    DOLABELLA   Heaven has but
    Our sorrow for our sins, and then delights
    To pardon erring man. Sweet mercy seems
8   Its darling attribute, which limits justice
    As if there were degrees in infinite,
    And infinite would rather want perfection
    Than punish to extent.

    ANTONY   I can forgive
9   A foe, but not a mistress and a friend.

Treason is there in its most horrid shape
Where trust is greatest, and the soul, resigned,
Is stabbed by its own guards. I'll hear no more.—
Hence from my sight forever!

CLEOPATRA   How? Forever?
I cannot go one moment from your sight,
And must I go forever?
My joys, my only joys, are centered here.
What place have I to go to? My own kingdom?
That I have lost for you. Or to the Romans?
They hate me for your sake. Or must I wander
The wide world o'er, a helpless, banished woman,
Banished for love of you—banished from you?
Aye, there's the banishment! Oh, hear me, hear me
With strictest justice, for I beg no favor,
And if I have offended you, then kill me,
But do not banish me.

ANTONY   I must not hear you.
I have a fool within me takes your part,
But honor stops my ears.

CLEOPATRA   For pity hear me!
Would you cast off a slave who followed you?
Who crouched beneath your spurn?—He has no pity!
See if he gives one tear to my departure,
One look, one kind farewell. O iron heart!
Let all the gods look down and judge betwixt us,
If he did ever love!

ANTONY   No more.—Alexas!

DOLABELLA A perjured villain!

ANTONY [to CLEOPATRA]   Your Alexas, yours.

CLEOPATRA Oh, 'twas his plot, his ruinous design,
T' engage you in my love by jealousy.
Hear him. Confront him with me. Let him speak.

ANTONY I have, I have.

CLEOPATRA   And if he clear me not—

ANTONY Your creature! one who hangs upon your smiles!
Watches your eye to say or to unsay
Whate'er you please! I am not to be moved.

CLEOPATRA Then must we part? Farewell, my cruel lord!
Th' appearance is against me, and I go,
Unjustified, forever from your sight.
How I have loved, you know; how yet I love,
My only comfort is, I know myself.

1   I love you more, even now you are unkind,
       Than when you loved me most; so well, so truly
       I'll never strive against it but die pleased
       To think you once were mine.

       ANTONY   Good heaven, they weep at parting!
2   Must I weep too? That calls them innocent.
       I must not weep. And yet I must, to think
       That I must not forgive.—
       Live, but live wretched; 'tis but just you should,
       Who made me so. Live from each other's sight.
       Let me not hear, you meet. Set all the earth
3   And all the seas betwixt your sundered loves;
       View nothing common but the sun and skies.
       Now, all take several ways;
       And each your own sad fate, with mine, deplore;
       That you were false, and I could trust no more.

4   [*Exeunt severally.*]

ACT FIVE

[C<small>LEOPATRA</small>, C<small>HARMION</small>, I<small>RAS</small>.] 1

C<small>HARMION</small> Be juster, Heaven; such virtue punished thus
  Will make us think that chance rules all above,
  And shuffles with a random hand the lots
  Which man is forced to draw.

C<small>LEOPATRA</small> I could tear out these eyes that gained his heart, 2
  And had not power to keep it. O the curse
  Of doting on, even when I find it dotage!
  Bear witness, gods, you heard him bid me go;
  You whom he mocked with imprecating vows
  Of promised faith!—I'll die! I will not bear it.
  You may hold me— 3

[*She pulls out her dagger, and they hold her.*]

  But I can keep my breath; I can die inward,
  And choke this love.

[*Enter* A<small>LEXAS</small>.] 4

I<small>RAS</small>   Help, O Alexas, help!
  The queen grows desperate; her soul struggles in her
  With all the agonies of love and rage,
  And strives to force its passage.

C<small>LEOPATRA</small>   Let me go. 5
  Art thou there, traitor!—Oh,
  Oh, for a little breath, to vent my rage!
  Give, give me way, and let me loose upon him.

A<small>LEXAS</small> Yes, I deserve it for my ill-timed truth.
  Was it for me to prop 6
  The ruins of a falling majesty?
  To place myself beneath the mighty flaw,
  Thus to be crushed and pounded into atoms
  By its o'erwhelming weight? 'Tis too presuming
  For subjects to preserve that wilful power 7
  Which courts its own destruction.

C<small>LEOPATRA</small>   I would reason
  More calmly with you. Did not you o'errule
  And force my plain, direct, and open love
  Into these crooked paths of jealousy?
  Now, what's the event? Octavia is removed, 8
  But Cleopatra's banished. Thou, thou villain,
  Hast pushed my boat to open sea, to prove

63

1 At my sad cost, if thou canst steer it back.
It cannot be; I'm lost too far; I'm ruined!—
Hence, thou imposter, traitor, monster, devil!—
I can no more. Thou, and my griefs, have sunk
Me down so low that I want voice to curse thee.

2 ALEXAS Suppose some shipwrecked seaman near the shore,
Dropping and faint with climbing up the cliff;
If, from above, some charitable hand
Pull him to safety, hazarding himself
To draw the other's weight, would he look back
And curse him for his pains? The case is yours;
3 But one step more, and you have gained the height.

CLEOPATRA Sunk, never more to rise.

ALEXAS Octavia's gone, and Dolabella banished.
Believe me, madam, Antony is yours.
His heart was never lost, but started off
4 To jealousy, love's last retreat and covert,
Where it lies hid in shades, watchful in silence,
And listening for the sound that calls it back.
Some other, any man ('tis so advanced)
May perfect this unfinished work, which I
5 (Unhappy only to myself) have left
So easy to his hand.

CLEOPATRA Look well thou do 't; else—

ALEXAS Else what your silence threatens.—Antony
Is mounted up the Pharos, from whose turret
6 He stands surveying our Egyptian galleys
Engaged with Caesar's fleet. Now death or conquest!
If the first happen, fate acquits my promise;
If we o'ercome, the conqueror is yours.

[A distant shout within.]

7

CHARMION Have comfort, madam. Did you mark that shout?

[Second shout nearer.]

IRAS Hark! they redouble it.

8 ALEXAS   'Tis from the port.
The loudness shows it near. Good news, kind heavens!

CLEOPATRA Osiris make it so!

[Enter SERAPION.]

9 SERAPION   Where, where's the queen?

ALEXAS   How frightfully the holy coward stares
   As if not yet recovered of the assault,
   When all his gods and, what's more dear to him,
   His offerings were at stake!

SERAPION   O horror, horror!
   Egypt has been; our latest hour is come;
   The queen of nations from her ancient seat
   Is sunk forever in the dark abyss;
   Time has unrolled her glories to the last,
   And now closed up the volume.

CLEOPATRA   Be more plain.
   Say whence thou comest, though fate is in thy face,
   Which from thy haggard eyes looks wildly out,
   And threatens ere thou speakest.

SERAPION   I came from Pharos—
   From viewing (spare me, and imagine it)
   Our land's last hope, your navy—

CLEOPATRA   Vanquished?

SERAPION   No.
   They fought not.

CLEOPATRA   Then they fled!

SERAPION   Nor that. I saw,
   With Antony, your well-appointed fleet
   Row out; and thrice he waved his hand on high,
   And thrice with cheerful cries they shouted back.
   'Twas then false Fortune like a fawning strumpet
   About to leave the bankrupt prodigal,
   With a dissembled smile would kiss at parting,
   And flatter to the last; the well-timed oars
   Now dipt from every bank, now smoothly run
   To meet the foe; and soon indeed they met,
   But not as foes. In few, we saw their caps
   On either side thrown up. The Egyptian galleys,
   Received like friends, passed through and fell behind
   The Roman rear. And now they all come forward,
   And ride within the port.

CLEOPATRA   Enough, Serapion.
   I've heard my doom.—This needed not, you gods:
   When I lost Antony, your work was done.
   'Tis but superfluous malice.—Where's my lord?
   How bears he this last blow?

SERAPION   His fury cannot be expressed by words.
   Thrice he attempted headlong to have fallen

1 Full on his foes, and aimed at Caesar's galley;
   Withheld, he raves on you; cries he's betrayed.
   Should he now find you—

ALEXAS   Shun him. Seek your safety
   Till you can clear your innocence.

2 CLEOPATRA   I'll stay.

ALEXAS You must not. Haste you to your monument,
   While I make speed to Caesar.

CLEOPATRA   Caesar! No,
   I have no business with him.

3
ALEXAS   I can work him
   To spare your life, and let this madman perish.

CLEOPATRA Base, fawning wretch! wouldst thou betray him too?
   Hence from my sight! I will not hear a traitor.
   'Twas thy design brought all this ruin on us.—
4 Serapion, thou art honest. Counsel me—
   But haste, each moment's precious.

SERAPION Retire. You must not yet see Antony.
   He who began this mischief,
   'Tis just he tempt the danger. Let him clear you;
5 And, since he offered you his servile tongue,
   To gain a poor precarious life from Caesar
   Let him expose that fawning eloquence,
   And speak to Antony.

ALEXAS   O heaven! I dare not;
6 I meet my certain death.

CLEOPATRA   Slave, thou deservest it.—
   Not that I fear my lord, will I avoid him;
   I know him noble. When he banished me,
   And thought me false, he scorned to take my life;
7 But I'll be justified, and then die with him.

ALEXAS O pity me, and let me follow you!

CLEOPATRA To death, if thou stir hence. Speak if thou canst
   Now for thy life which basely thou wouldst save,
   While mine I prize at—this. Come, good Serapion.

8 [Exeunt CLEOPATRA, SERAPION, CHARMION, and IRAS.]

ALEXAS O that I less could fear to lose this being,
   Which, like a snowball in my coward hand,
   The more 'tis grasped, the faster melts away.
   Poor reason! what a wretched aid art thou!
9 For still, in spite of thee,

These two long lovers, soul and body, dread
Their final separation. Let me think;
What can I say to save myself from death,
No matter what becomes of Cleopatra?

ANTONY [*within*]   Which way? where?

VENTIDIUS [*within*]   This leads to the monument.

ALEXAS   Ah me! I hear him; yet I'm unprepared,
   My gift of lying's gone;
   And this court-devil, which I so oft have raised,
   Forsakes me at my need. I dare not stay,
   Yet cannot far go hence. [*Exit.*]

[*Enter* ANTONY *and* VENTIDIUS.]

ANTONY   O happy Caesar! thou hast men to lead!
   Think not 'tis thou hast conquered Antony,
   But Rome has conquered Eygpt. I'm betrayed.

VENTIDIUS   Curse on this treacherous train!
   Their soil and heaven infect them all with baseness,
   And their young souls come tainted to the world
   With the first breath they draw.

ANTONY   The original villain sure no god created;
   He was a bastard of the sun by Nile,
   Aped into man; with all his mother's mud
   Crusted about his soul.

VENTIDIUS   The nation is
   One universal traitor, and their queen
   The very spirit and extract of them all.

ANTONY   Is there yet left
   A possibility of aid from valor?
   Is there one god unsworn to my destruction?
   The least unmortgaged hope? for, if there be,
   Methinks I cannot fall beneath the fate
   Of such a boy as Caesar.
   The world's one half is yet in Antony,
   And from each limb of it that's hewed away,
   The soul comes back to me.

VENTIDIUS   There yet remain
   Three legions in the town. The last assault
   Lopt off the rest. If death be your design—
   As I must wish it now—these are sufficient
   To make a heap about us of dead foes,
   An honest pile for burial.

ANTONY   They're enough.

1   We'll not divide our stars, but, side by side,
    Fight emulous, and with malicious eyes
    Survey each other's acts, so every death
    Thou giv'st, I'll take on me as a just debt,
    And pay thee back a soul.

2   VENTIDIUS   Now you shall see I love you. Not a word
    Of chiding more. By my few hours of life,
    I am so pleased with this brave Roman fate
    That I would not be Caesar to outlive you.
    When we put off this flesh and mount together,
    I shall be shown to all the ethereal crowd,—
3   "Lo, this is he who died with Antony!"

ANTONY   Who knows but we may pierce through all their troops,
    And reach my veterans yet? 'tis worth the 'tempting
    To o'erleap this gulf of fate,
    And leave our wondering destinies behind.

4   [*Enter* ALEXAS, *trembling.*]

VENTIDIUS   See, see, that villain!
    See Cleopatra stamped upon that face
    With all her cunning, all her arts of falsehood!
    How she looks out through those dissembling eyes!
5   How he has set his count'nance for deceit,
    And promises a lie before he speaks!

[*drawing*]

    Let me dispatch him first.

6   ALEXAS   O spare me, spare me!

ANTONY   Hold! He's not worth your killing.—On thy life,
    Which thou may'st keep because I scorn to take it,
    No syllable to justify thy queen.
    Save thy base tongue its office.

7   ALEXAS   Sir, she's gone
    Where she shall never be molested more
    By love, or you.

ANTONY   Fled to her Dolabella!
    Die, traitor! I revoke my promise! die! [*going to kill him.*]

8   ALEXAS   O hold! she is not fled.

ANTONY   She is. My eyes
    Are open to her falsehood; my whole life
    Has been a golden dream of love and friendship;
    But, now I wake, I'm like a merchant roused
9   From soft repose to see his vessel sinking,

And all his wealth cast o'er. Ingrateful woman!   1
Who followed me but as the swallow summer,
Hatching her young ones in my kindly beams,
Singing her flatteries to my morning wake;
But now my winter comes, she spreads her wings,
And seeks the spring of Caesar.   2

ALEXAS   Think not so:
Her fortunes have in all things mixed with yours.
Had she betrayed her naval force to Rome,
How easily might she have gone to Caesar,
Secure by such a bribe.   3

VENTIDIUS   She sent it first,
To be more welcome after.

ANTONY   'Tis too plain,
Else would she have appeared to clear herself.

ALEXAS   Too fatally she has. She could not bear   4
To be accused by you, but shut herself
Within her monument, looked down and sighed,
While from her unchanged face the silent tears
Dropped, as they had not leave, but stole their parting.
Some undistinguished words she inly murmured;
At last she raised her eyes, and, with such looks   5
As dying Lucrece cast—

ANTONY   My heart forebodes—

VENTIDIUS   All for the best;—go on.

ALEXAS   She snatched her poniard,   6
And, ere we could prevent the fatal blow,
Plunged it within her breast, then turned to me:
"Go, bear my lord," said she, "my last farewell,
And ask him if he yet suspect my faith."
More she was saying, but death rushed betwixt.
She half pronounced your name with her last breath,   7
And buried half within her.

VENTIDIUS   Heaven be praised!

ANTONY   Then art thou innocent, my poor dear love?
And art thou dead?
O those two words! their sound should be divided;   8
Hadst thou been false, and died; or hadst thou lived,
And hadst been true—But innocence and death!
This shows not well above. Then what am I,
The murderer of this truth, this innocence!
Thoughts cannot form themselves in words so horrid   9
As can express my guilt!

1   VENTIDIUS Is 't come to this? The gods have been too gracious,
And thus you thank 'em for 't!

ANTONY [*to* ALEXAS]   Why stayest thou here?
Is it for thee to spy upon my soul
And see its inward mourning? Get thee hence.
2   Thou art not worthy to behold what now
Becomes a Roman emperor to perform.

ALEXAS [*aside*] He loves her still:
His grief betrays it. Good! the joy to find
She's yet alive completes the reconcilement.
I've saved myself and her. But, oh! the Romans!
3   Fate comes too fast upon my wit,
Hunts me too hard, and meets me at each double. [*Exit.*]

VENTIDIUS Would she had died a little sooner, though,
Before Octavia went; you might have treated;
Now 'twill look tame, and would not be received.
4   Come, rouse yourself, and let's die warm together.

ANTONY I will not fight: there's no more work for war.
The business of my angry hours is done.

VENTIDIUS Caesar is at your gates.

5   ANTONY   Why, let him enter;
He's welcome now.

VENTIDIUS What lethargy has crept into your soul?

ANTONY 'Tis but a scorn of life, and just desire
To free myself from bondage.

6   VENTIDIUS   Do it bravely.

ANTONY I will; but not by fighting. O Ventidius!
What should I fight for now?—my queen is dead.
I was but great for her; my power, my empire,
Were but my merchandise to buy her love,
7   And conquered kings, my factors. Now she's dead,
Let Caesar take the world,—
An empty circle since the jewel's gone
Which made it worth my strife; my being's nauseous;
For all the bribes of life are gone away.

8   VENTIDIUS Would you be taken?

ANTONY   Yes, I would be taken,
But as a Roman ought,—dead, my Ventidius.
For I'll convey my soul from Caesar's reach,
And lay down life myself. 'Tis time the world
Should have a lord, and know whom to obey.
9   We two have kept its homage in suspense,

And bent the globe, on whose each side we trod,　　　　　　　1
Till it was dinted inwards. Let him walk
Alone upon 't; I'm weary of my part.
My torch is out; and the world stands before me
Like a black desert at th' approach of night.
I'll lay me down and stray no farther on.　　　　　　　　　2

VENTIDIUS　　I could be grieved,
But that I'll not outlive you. Choose your death,
For I have seen him in such various shapes,
I care not which I take—I'm only troubled,
The life I bear is worn to such a rag,
'Tis scarce worth giving. I could wish, indeed,　　　　　　3
We threw it from us with a better grace;
That, like two lions taken in the toils,
We might at least thrust out our paws and wound
The hunters that inclose us.

ANTONY　　　　　　　　　I have thought on it.　　　4
Ventidius, you must live.

VENTIDIUS　　　　　　　I must not, sir.

ANTONY　Wilt thou not live to speak some good of me?
To stand by my fair fame and guard the approaches
From the ill tongues of men?　　　　　　　　　　　　5

VENTIDIUS　　　　　　　Who shall guard mine
For living after you?

ANTONY　　　　　　Say I command it.

VENTIDIUS　　If we die well, our deaths will speak themselves,
And need no living witness.　　　　　　　　　　　　6

ANTONY　　　　　　　　Thou hast loved me,
And fain I would reward thee. I must die.
Kill me, and take the merit of my death
To make thee friends with Caesar.

VENTIDIUS　　　　　　　Thank your kindness.　　7
You said I loved you; and in recompense
You bid me turn a traitor.—Did I think
You would have used me thus?—that I should die
With a hard thought of you?

ANTONY　　　　　　　Forgive me, Roman.　　　8
Since I have heard of Cleopatra's death,
My reason bears no rule upon my tongue,
But lets my thought break all at random out.
I've thought better; do not deny me twice.

VENTIDIUS　　By Heaven, I will not.　　　　　　　9
Let it not be to outlive you.

1   ANTONY   Kill me first,
     And then die thou; for 'tis but just thou serve
     Thy friend before thyself.

   VENTIDIUS   Give me your hand.
     We soon shall meet again. Now farewell, emperor!—

2   *[embrace]*

     Methinks that word's too cold to be my last:
     Since death sweeps all distinctions, farewell, friend!
     That's all—
     I will not make a business of a trifle;
3   And yet I cannot look on you and kill you;
     Pray turn your face.

   ANTONY   I do. Strike home, be sure.

   VENTIDIUS   Home as my sword will reach. [*Kills himself.*]

   ANTONY   Oh, thou mistak'st;
4   That wound was none of thine; give it me back;
     Thou robb'st me of my death.

   VENTIDIUS   I do, indeed;
     But think 'tis the first time I e'er deceived you,
     If that may plead my pardon.—And you, gods,
5   Forgive me if you will; for I die perjured
     Rather than kill my friend. [*Dies.*]

   ANTONY   Farewell! Ever my leader, even in death!
     My queen and thou have got the start of me,
     And I'm the lag of honor.—Gone so soon?
     Is death no more? he used him carelessly,
6   With a familiar kindness; ere he knocked,
     Ran to the door and took him in his arms,
     As who should say, "You're welcome at all hours,
     A friend need give no warning." Books had spoiled him,
     For all the learn'd are cowards by profession.
7   'Tis not worth
     My farther thought; for death, for aught I know,
     Is but to think no more. Here's to be satisfied. [*falls on his sword*]
     I've missed my heart. O unperforming hand!
     Thou never couldst have erred in a worse time.
     My fortune jades me to the last; and death,
8   Like a great man, takes state, and makes me wait
     For my admittance—

   [trampling within]

                     Some, perhaps, from Caesar
     If he should find me living, and suspect
9   That I played booty with my life! I'll mend

My work ere they can reach me. [*rises upon his knees*]   1

[*Enter* CLEOPATRA, CHARMION, IRAS.]

CLEOPATRA   Where is my lord? where is he?

CHARMION   There he lies,
And dead Ventidius by him.   2

CLEOPATRA   My fears were prophets; I am come too late. [*runs to him*]
  O that accursed Alexas!

ANTONY   Art thou living?
Or am I dead before I knew, and thou   3
The first kind ghost that meets me?

CLEOPATRA   Help me seat him.
Send quickly, send for help!

[*They place him in a chair.*]

     4

ANTONY   I am answered.
We live both. Sit thee down, my Cleopatra;
I'll make the most I can of life, to stay
A moment more with thee.

CLEOPATRA   How is it with you?

     5

ANTONY   'Tis as with a man
Removing in a hurry; all packed up,
But one dear jewel that his haste forgot;
And he, for that, returns upon the spur;
So I come back for thee.

CLEOPATRA   Too long, you heavens, you have been cruel to me;   6
Now show your mended faith, and give me back
His fleeting life!

ANTONY   It will not be, my love;
I keep my soul by force.
Say but, thou are not false.   7

CLEOPATRA   'Tis now too late
To say I'm true: I'll prove it, and die with you.
Unknown to me, Alexas feigned my death,
Which, when I knew, I hastened to prevent
This fatal consequence. My fleet betrayed   8
Both you and me.

ANTONY   And Dolabella—

CLEOPATRA   Scarce
Esteemed before he loved; but hated now.

ANTONY   Enough. My life's not long enough for more.   9

1   Thou say'st thou wilt come after: I believe thee,
    For I can now believe whate'er thou sayest,
    That we may part more kindly.

    CLEOPATRA   I will come.
    Doubt not, my life, I'll come, and quickly too;
2   Caesar shall triumph o'er no part of thee.

    ANTONY   But grieve not, while thou stay'st,
    My last disastrous times.
    Think we have had a clear and glorious day,
    And Heaven did kindly to delay the storm
    Just till our close of evening. Ten years' love,
3   And not a moment lost, but all improved
    To the utmost joys,—what ages have we lived!
    And now to die each other's; and, so dying,
    While hand in hand, we walk in groves below,
    Whole troops of lovers' ghosts shall flock about us,
4   And all the train be ours.

    CLEOPATRA   Your words are like the notes of dying swans,
    Too sweet to last. Were there so many hours
    For your unkindness, and not one for love?

    ANTONY   No, not a minute.—This one kiss—more worth
    Than all I leave to Caesar. [*Dies.*]
5
    CLEOPATRA   O tell me so again,
    And take ten thousand kisses for that word.
    My lord, my lord! Speak, if you yet have being;
    Sign to me, if you cannot speak; or cast
    One look! Do anything that shows you live.
6
    IRAS   He's gone too far to hear you,
    And this you see, a lump of senseless clay,
    The leavings of a soul.

    CHARMION   Remember, madam,
7   He charged you not to grieve.

    CLEOPATRA   And I'll obey him.
    I have not loved a Roman not to know
    What should become his wife—his wife, my Charmion!
    For 'tis to that high title I aspire,
    And now I'll not die less. Let dull Octavia
8   Survive to mourn him, dead. My nobler fate
    Shall knit our spousals with a tie too strong
    For Roman laws to break.

    IRAS   Will you then die?

9   CLEOPATRA   Why shouldst thou make that question?

    IRAS   Caesar is merciful.

CLEOPATRA   Let him be so
  To those that want his mercy. My poor lord
  Made no such covenant with him to spare me
  When he was dead. Yield me to Caesar's pride?
  What! to be led in triumph through the streets,
  A spectacle to base plebeian eyes,
  While some dejected friend of Antony's
  Close in a corner, shakes his head, and mutters
  A secret curse on her who ruined him?
  I'll none of that.

CHARMION   Whatever you resolve,
  I'll follow, even to death.

IRAS   I only feared
  For you, but more should fear to live without you.

CLEOPATRA   Why, now, 'tis as it should be. Quick, my friends,
  Dispatch. Ere this, the town's in Caesar's hands.
  My lord looks down concerned, and fears my stay,
  Lest I should be surprised.
  Keep him not waiting for his love too long.
  You, Charmion, bring my crown and richest jewels;
  With them, the wreath of victory I made
  (Vain augury!) for him who now lies dead.
  You, Iras, bring the cure of all our ills.

IRAS   The aspics, madam?

CLEOPATRA   Must I bid you twice?

[*Exeunt* CHARMION *and* IRAS.]

  'Tis sweet to die when they would force life on me,
  To rush into the dark abode of death,
  And seize him first. If he be like my love,
  He is not frightful, sure.
  We're now alone in secrecy and silence;
  And is not this like lovers? I may kiss
  These pale, cold lips; Octavia does not see me.
  And oh! 'tis better far to have him thus
  Than see him in her arms.—Oh, welcome, welcome!

[*Enter* CHARMION *and* IRAS.]

CHARMION   What must be done?

CLEOPATRA   Short ceremony, friends,
  But yet it must be decent. First, this laurel
  Shall crown my hero's head; he fell not basely,
  Nor left his shield behind him.—Only thou
  Couldst triumph o'er thyself; and thou alone
  Wert worthy so to triumph.

1 CHARMION   To what end
  These ensigns of your pomp and royalty?

CLEOPATRA   Dull that thou art! why, 'tis to meet my love
As when I saw him first on Cydnos' bank,
All sparkling, like a goddess; so adorned,
2 I'll find him once again. My second spousals
Shall match my first in glory. Haste, haste, both,
And dress the bride of Antony.

CHARMION   —'Tis done.

CLEOPATRA   Now seat me by my lord. I claim this place,
For I must conquer Caesar, too, like him,
3 And win my share o' th' world.—Hail, you dear relics
Of my immortal love!
O let no impious hand remove you hence,
But rest forever here! Let Egypt give
His death that peace which it denied his life.—
4 Reach me the casket.

IRAS   Underneath the fruit
The aspic lies.

CLEOPATRA   Well, thou kind deceiver! [*putting aside the leaves*]
Thou best of thieves, who, with an easy key,
5 Dost open life and, unperceived by us,
Even steal us from ourselves, discharging so
Death's dreadful office better than himself,
Touching our limbs so gently into slumber
That Death stands by, deceived by his own image,
6 And thinks himself but sleep.

SERAPION [*within*]   The queen, where is she?
The town is yielded, Caesar's at the gates.

CLEOPATRA   He comes too late to invade the rights of death.
Haste, bare my arm, and rouse the serpent's fury. [*holds out her
7   arm, and draws it back*]
Coward flesh,
Wouldst thou conspire with Caesar to betray me
As thou wert none of mine? I'll force thee to 't,
And not be sent by him,
But bring, myself, my soul to Antony. [*turns aside, and then
8   shows her arm bloody*]
Take hence. The work is done.

SERAPION [*within*]   Break ope the door
And guard the traitor well.

CHARMION   The next is ours.
9 IRAS   Now, Charmion, to be worthy

Of our great queen and mistress.   1

[*They apply the aspics.*]

CLEOPATRA   Already, death, I feel thee in my veins.
   I go with such a will to find my lord
   That we shall quickly meet.
   A heavy numbness creeps through every limb,   2
   And now 'tis at my head. My eyelids fall,
   And my dear love is vanished in a mist.—
   Where shall I find him—where? O turn me to him,
   And lay me on his breast!—Caesar, thy worst.
   Now part us, if thou canst. [*Dies.*]
                                                         3

[IRAS *sinks down at her feet, and dies;* CHARMION *stands behind her
   chair, as dressing her head.*]

[*Enter* SERAPION, *two* PRIESTS, ALEXAS, *bound, and* EGYPTIANS.]

PRIEST   Behold, Serapion,
   What havoc death has made!   4

SERAPION   'Twas what I feared.—
   Charmion, is this well done?

CHARMION   Yes, 'tis well done, and like a queen, the last
   Of her great race. I follow her. [*sinks down; dies*]
                                                         5
ALEXAS   'Tis true,
   She has done well. Much better thus to die
   Than live to make a holiday in Rome.

SERAPION   See, see how the lovers sit in state together,
   As they were giving laws to half mankind!
   Th' impression of a smile, left in her face,   6
   Shows she died pleased with him for whom she lived,
   And went to charm him in another world.
   Caesar's just entering; grief has now no leisure.
   Secure that villain as our pledge of safety
   To grace the imperial triumph.—Sleep, blest pair,   7
   Secure from human chance, long ages out,
   While all the storms of fate fly o'er your tomb;
   And fame to late posterity shall tell,
   No lovers lived so great or died so well.

[*Exeunt.*]   8

EPILOGUE

1 Poets, like disputants when reasons fail,
  Have one sure refuge left—and that's to rail.
  Fop, coxcomb, fool, are thundered through the pit;
  And this is all their equipage of wit.
  We wonder how the devil this difference grows
  Betwixt our fools in verse, and yours in prose;

2 For, 'faith, the quarrel rightly understood,
  'Tis civil war with their own flesh and blood.
  The threadbare author hates the gaudy coat;
  And swears at the gilt coach, but swears afoot;
  For 'tis observed of every scribbling man,

3 He grows a fop as fast as e'er he can;
  Prunes up, and asks his oracle, the glass,
  If pink or purple best become his face.
  For our poor wretch, he neither rails nor prays;
  Nor likes your wit just as you like his plays;
  He has not yet so much of Mr. Bayes.

4 He does his best; and if he cannot please,
  Would quickly sue out his writ of ease.
  Yet, if he might his own grand jury call,
  By the fair sex he begs to stand or fall.
  Let Caesar's power the men's ambition move,
  But grace you him who lost the world for love!

5 Yet if some antiquated lady say,
  The last age is not copied in his play;
  Heaven help the man who for that face must drudge,
  Which only has the wrinkles of a judge.
  Let not the young and beauteous join with those;

6 For should you raise such numerous hosts of foes,
  Young wits and sparks he to his aid must call;
  'Tis more than one man's work to please you all.

7

78